P9-DHC-323

Free-Range Knitter

the yarn harlot writes again

stephanie pearl-mcphee

**Andrews McMeel
Publishing, LLC**

Kansas City

For my Uncle Tupper,
who taught me that intelligence and insight can occasionally be faked,
provided you are willing to replace them with really hard work.

Free-Range Knitter copyright © 2008 by Stephanie Pearl-McPhee. All rights reserved.
Printed in the United States of America. No part of this book may be used or reproduced
in any manner whatsoever without written permission except in the case of reprints in
the context of reviews. For information, write Andrews McMeel Publishing, LLC, an
Andrews McMeel Universal company, 1130 Walnut Street, Kansas City, Missouri 64106.

08 09 10 11 12 RR2 10 9 8 7 6 5 4

Library of Congress Cataloging-in-Publication Data
Pearl-McPhee, Stephanie.
    Free-range knitter : the yarn harlot writes again / Stephanie Pearl-McPhee. —1st ed.
      p. cm.
    ISBN-13: 978-0-7407-6947-4
    ISBN-10: 0-7407-6947-2
  1. Knitting—Miscellanea. 2. Knitting—Humor. 3. Knitter (Persons)—Miscellanea. I.
Title.

TT820.P372 2008
746.43'2—dc22

2008026849

Book design by Holly Camerlinck
www.andrewsmcmeel.com

Attention: Schools and Businesses

Andrews McMeel books are available at quantity discounts with bulk purchase for
educational, business, or sales promotional use. For information, please write to: Special
Sales Department, Andrews McMeel Publishing, LLC, 1130 Walnut Street, Kansas City,
Missouri 64106.

CONTENTS

CHAPTER 3

CHAPTER 4

CHAPTER 5

CHAPTER 6

CHAPTER 7

ACKNOWLEDGMENTS

I am enormously grateful to the people who have made this book possible by laughing, thinking, listening, knitting, and reading:

The fine people at Andrews McMeel Publishing, specifically my editor, Katherine Anderson. Their ability to see possibility where others see an oddity means a great deal to me.

My agent and friend Linda Roghaar, for everything—and then some.

My steady husband, Joe, and my remarkable daughters, Amanda, Megan, and Sam. This book wouldn't be what it is without the time alone in the woods. Thanks for giving me that and so much more.

My family: Bonnie, Erin, Ian, Ali, Hank, Tupper, Susan, Ken, Carol, Joe, Kelly, Katie, Chris, Robyn, Ben . . . You are all inspiration and fodder. Thank you.

My friends Rachel, Cass, Denny, Megan, Lene, Tina . . . and so many more. Your support and validation is invaluable. I wouldn't be me without you.

Every knitter I ever met. You're all something else.

INTRODUCTION

I have been in the definitely odd and sometimes enviable position of having been on a knitting book tour (sometimes I call it a yarn crawl) for roughly the last two years. Obviously, I'm not on tour every minute of every day, but I do spend a completely unreasonable amount of time wandering from city to city all over North America talking to knitters. Since I'm not a teacher, just a knitting philosopher of sorts, I don't necessarily have a reason for being there. I have no agenda, I don't promote one sort of knitting or some particular patterns, I don't sell yarn. I'm just there to sign humor books about knitting, meet knitters, drink beer with them, observe them in their natural habitat (the local yarn shop), scrutinize them as they vacation at fiber festivals and conferences, and talk to them as I discover them in the wild.

Book tours (even knitting book tours) move really fast. So fast that a typical day involves getting up at an ungodly hour, going to the airport of whatever city I'm in, knitting while I wait to be flown to another city, knitting while I fly to another city, knitting on the way to the hotel, unpacking and showering in the hotel, knitting in the cab on the way to the speaking engagement (about knitting, and usually in a yarn shop), meeting all the knitters, and then sleeping (briefly) before I do it again in another city the next day. If you wanted to meet as many knitters as possible there would be no better way to do it, though as I'm sure you can imagine, the city you are in starts to be irrelevant after a couple of days, enough so that you forget to find out where you are. Doing the same thing every day while being constantly surrounded by only yarn, knitters, and knitting for days on end gives me an odd perspective. Since I often lose track of what city (state or province) I am in, it removes the idea that geography matters and leaves me with the odd impression that I am traveling a world where only knitting matters, all the people are knitters, and all the stores sell yarn.

Following the logic here, visiting more than fifty yarn stores and guilds a year means that I meet a lot of knitters, I get a lot of material about knitting, I see knitters without the boundaries of politics and geography (mostly because I am completely freaking lost), and I buy a lot of yarn, which is another problem and another story for another day, but for the record, totally not my fault. I'm only human. (Who among you can throw the first stone? Even if you only fell down and bought yarn at half of the shops, wouldn't you still have a really big problem?) This constant exposure to yarn, patterns, needles, and yarn shops of all kinds lends another set of insights: our stuff and what we do with it.

I have then, as a passionate knitter, a knitting book writer, a knitting traveler, and a compatriot of the knitting masses, spent a lot of time thinking about knitting and knitters. I definitely think about knitting and knitters more than most people, which I guess isn't that hard, since I have recently confirmed an ugly truth that explains a great deal: Most people aren't thinking about knitting or knitters at all.

This book, then, is what I think knitters are thinking. Some of these stories are true. Some are mostly true. Some have names changed to protect the innocent, and in some cases, names have been written down perfectly to glorify the clever. This book shares stories of knitting triumph and failure, knitting success and defeat, lessons missed and lessons learned. This book is about the things we have in common, we knitters, no matter where we live, whom we love, or what we are knitting. This book is what I'm using to prove to my family that I may be completely out of my mind with this knitting thing, but I have a lot of friends just like me. This book is about yarn. This book is about needles. This book is about the truth about the way things are.

This book, though it appears to be about knitting, is actually about knitters.

CHAPTER 1

Cast On

Stories of Beginnings, Good Starts, Optimism,
and Hope Springing (Mostly) Eternal

Annabelle

Annabelle is four, almost five years old, and she is knitting. Sitting on the very edge of an old, once-blue, upholstered chair, she couldn't possibly be working with a greater degree of focus. Her hair is golden and tousled, hanging in loose curls, and her downcast eyes, hidden under devastatingly long lashes, are a beautiful, warm light brown that always makes me think of toffee and topaz. I know that somewhere within you must reside certain stereotypes, maybe born of childhood readings of *Little Women* or a Jane Austen novel, and that those ideas mean that you have begun to form opinions and have visions about the sort of little girl who would be sitting still and enjoying knitting. Maybe these ideas have already helped you begin dressing Annabelle and that, in your mind's eye, you've got her wearing something like a pinafore or a velvet dress with lace ruffles and some small buttons.

Let go of that idea right now, because although Annabelle (she prefers Annie) is currently sitting and knitting, and she is indeed quiet, concentrating, and peaceful, she is also clad in an outfit of her own choosing, which she began with a pair of gathered flannel green and black plaid pants, complemented with a yellow top with lace sleeves, and accessorized with two necklaces cleverly concocted of macaroni and a rainbow of beads. To round out the look she has donned a ripped raincoat and a purple wool hat her mother knit that is supposed to have dinosaur spikes on it, but Annie has decided it more resembles a crown. She is only wearing one sock, and there is just no way to know where the other one is. (As long as all of the motors in the house's major appliances are still working and I don't smell smoke, then I have decided that I'm not going to worry about where it might be.)

There are other clues to Annie's basic nature, for those astute enough to notice. There is a very large smear of sparkle glue on the arm of the chair she's sitting in and what may be dried ketchup or blood (or both) on the other. One wall behind this chair is covered in several vibrant works of graffiti art, which center almost entirely around the expressive use of the letter A. (Remind me to give Annie a little tip later: Never sign your name when defiling something; it makes excellent evidence for the prosecution.) Down the hall there is an entire roll of unwound toilet paper that I haven't cleaned up yet, and frankly, if I keep her alive (and from setting fire to that roll or trying to flush it down the toilet in one big wad) until her mother comes back, I will feel that I have done an excellent job while babysitting.

As you may be beginning to suspect, Annie is not the sort of child you would expect to be knitting. In fact, she's the opposite type. Annie is fast moving, dirty, bright, thrill seeking, and loud. She's the exact sort of child that people are always pointing out to me as an

I'm not charmed just by Annie's knitting but because it's being done by Annie herself. I feel that Annie and I have a connection, an understanding of sorts, and it is not only because she's knitting, or because my mother would be happy to tell you that I was the same sort of kid (talking it through is part of her recovery program). Annabelle bears a real resemblance to my eldest daughter, Amanda, and not just because two hours ago she liberated her hamster and set off an incident involving the cat and the toaster that will likely take another hour off her poor mother's life. Like Amanda, Annie is a seriously challenging kid. Whatever you're thinking a regular kid is, Annie is just more. If she's happy, she's the happiest kid ever. If she's angry, you will be stunned at the degree of fury her petite body can throw your way. If she's doing something and is determined about it, she'll define determination, and if she wants something, she will pursue it with a passion and dedication that could bring a veteran grandmother of twelve to her knees.

I'm here; babysitting Annie, because her mother has the same problem that I did when I was trying to raise my first child. Only a seasoned professional parent can take the heat these intense kids can dish out, and usually the only thing a mother with a child like this can do is to opt not to leave her side until she can be trusted not to take out a sixteen-year-old babysitter who let her guard down for a moment. (I once had three police cars show up because my novice babysitter had made the foolish mistake of going to the bathroom for a tissue. In the seventy-nine seconds it took her to blow her nose, my darling and intrepid three-year-old had dialed 911 and then hung up.

The guileless sitter was none the wiser until moments later, when six cops were bashing on the door shouting, "What is the nature of your emergency?") Annie's mother, Ruth, had been trying to avoid just such an event by supervising her canny progeny herself and trusting no one until Annabelle was less of a danger to herself and others, but the projected twelve years became a long time to go without a dental cleaning. Ruth had tried taking Annie with her the last time, but after the firemen had left the clinic and the gas leak had been repaired, the dentist had suggested to her that she lose his number until she found Annie a babysitter. Enter me and my experience.

My daughter Amanda's specialty was stripping. (She minored in volume and its applications in the art of persuasion, another field in which she excelled.) My kid, wearing a full set of clothes and a full-body zip-up snowsuit with boots, could go from being fully clad and restrained in her stroller's five-point harness system to absolutely stark naked and running the store like a wild animal in the amount of time my back was turned to pay the clerk. I spent years wrestling a naked, furious, and occasionally wet toddler back into clothes in all manner of public places. I could never figure out how she did it, and I still have a special fondness for dressing kids in tights, layers, and overalls, as they were the strategies that seemed to slow Amanda down, even a little. (Should you have a similar strip artist at home, know that she is now eighteen and seems to have outgrown the urge, which has been a tremendous relief. For a while there I worried it would end up being her job.)

Annie, on the other hand, specializes in escape and liberation.

(Like Amanda, Annie has also chosen not to limit herself and works at a subspecialty of destruction and vandalism.) Annabelle unties dogs, opens cages, releases ferrets, and has poured fish in the pasta water. She removes babies from cribs where they have been wrongly incarcerated, serving under the cruel régime of naptime, which Annie herself has seldom succumbed to. (Like many intense and challenging kids, she seems to need less sleep than her parents.) Continuing the liberation theme, Annie will, if the possibility presents, instantly make a break for it herself. She has gone missing everywhere her mother has taken her for the last four years, and from the moment in her infancy that she gained the ability to roll over, and thereby roll away, her mother has spent half of every day saying, "Where the hell is Annabelle?"

Despite the obvious downsides to trying to parent a kid like this (constant vigilance takes its toll), I actually think that having a kid of this type is a wonderful thing. (I think this especially now that mine has grown up without either of us going to prison, and I have accepted the premature aging, gray hair, and twitch over my right eye as necessary costs for her survival to maturity.) I like kids who are hard like this in general, and I like Annie in specific, because I've come to believe that a lot of challenging behavior in kids comes about as a result of these particular little ankle biters being too darn smart for their own good, and I have respect for that, just because I knit.

It is my considered belief that the number one reason knitters knit is because they are so smart that they need knitting to make boring things interesting. Knitters are so compellingly clever that they simply can't tolerate boredom. It takes more to engage and we've turned to knitting as a tool instead of other, more coarse coping techniques. The cruel truth is that kangaroos under stress will remove young from their pouches and abandon them, that some birds will eat their very own eggs if they are overcrowded, and that some overwhelmed and inexperienced hamster mothers have been known to kill and eat their own young. Ruth and I (along with any mother who has ever had a kid whose nickname was "Houdini" or "The Volcano") should give ourselves a little pat on the back each and every day that despite being very much under stress, profoundly inexperienced, and helplessly overcrowded, we have turned to no such maternal crimes, although I think if you got us a glass of wine or two we would all be happy to tell you that we certainly understand the urge. Instead, clever parents that we are, we took a kid like Annie, a kid who ten minutes ago was trying to shave all the fur off the cat to make her more comfortable in the summer heat, and we taught her to knit.

The best part is that we don't think of it as a tool we're giving our kids to cope with their extraordinary and potent natures for the rest of their lives, and we don't think of it as a way to help them learn to manage their intensity. No, no, my knitterly friends, as I look at wee Annabelle, who has been sitting in one place and knitting quietly for a whole seven minutes now, no, no. We think of it, now that those seven minutes have elapsed without our kids trying to take apart the stereo, paint with glue, or escape the confines of their homes, as pure, unadulterated, and mercenary self-defense.

Dear Designer #1

Dear Designer,

I want you to know that I'm very much enjoying your beautiful sock pattern. The panels down the sides of the legs are fetching and rather remind me of wings, if wings were stacked on top of each other, which they almost never are, but you know what I mean. I knew the moment that I saw it that this design was exactly what I was looking for and that my search for the perfect sock pattern to use with this particular yarn was over.

I really love it. It is perfection in and of itself, and I have no idea or explanation for why I was compelled to ~~bastardize modify~~ personalize the design. I believe I have a disease for which I cannot be held accountable. I stood there and talked about how darn ideal this pattern was, and then despite my every intention to just haul off and knit it, I lost control of myself. It appears now that I am incapable of knitting a pattern all the way through without changing something—even if, and I stress this, even if there is absolutely nothing lacking in the pattern whatsoever.

I have modified the finest Aran sweaters in the land (they tend to be a little wide for my frame, and I don't care for bobbles—no offense intended), and I have altered classic Norwegian colorwork sweaters that have stood the test of time and been knit millions of times by perfectly satisfied knitters who didn't find them at all wanting. (The neck was a smidge too round. I can't believe no one has noticed before me.)

I tell you all this as a way of explaining that I am an equal opportunity despoiler, that I do not discriminate on the basis of reputation, talent, or design experience. Nay, I feel free to mess with any and all patterns that strike me as needing a little improvement. If it is any comfort to you at all, these improvements frequently result in a certain *je ne sais quoi* that renders the garment unwearable, so perhaps you shall have your revenge yet, when I alter my way right out of a pair of socks that can be worn on human feet. In any case, I didn't want you to think that this was in any way personal, which it certainly was not.

There's nothing wrong with your design. It needed nothing done to it at all, and I didn't want you to take my string of rampant alterations personally. It means nothing that I have changed everything, except that I am a difficult person with odd taste. Again, I beg your forgiveness. I would tell you that I'll try to stop, but I'd be lying. And I don't want that to be between us.

In the spirit of that honesty, I do feel that you have a right to know what I have done with this pattern, the fruit of your needles, and I have enclosed a photo. It is best that you see this, since I have a terrible habit of telling people that it is so-and-so's pattern (in this case, yours) even though I have altered it beyond recognition. (Again, I feel dreadful about this, but until there is some sort of recovery program for me I think it somewhat likely that both of us will continue to be tormented by my behavior, and warning you up front and admitting to my faults is all I can do.) Please don't take any of this personally; the work was indefectible, masterful, and sublime before I took a fancy to it.

Thank you,
Stephanie

P.S.: I have also taken to referring to the panels as "openwork" rather than using the term "lace." These socks are to be a gift for my brother, and I think it sounds more masculine.

P.P.S.: After I changed the stitch count, reworked the heel, continued the panels, and opted to widen the panel, the stitch count isn't quite working for the toe decreases. Please advise.

Glory Days

I knit in the summer. All the way through the hot, steamy days, wool slips on my rather sweaty needles. Although Canadians are a northern people, and the summer here is very short, it can be so hot that it seems to produce a sort of amnesia in us. People come up to me while I'm knitting this time of year, and they stare like they can scarcely believe it's happening. "Isn't it a little hot for a hat?" they quip, and I get where they are coming from. The long and dark Canadian winter demands a certain fortitude, and the only way to build that fortitude is to have a few months where we deny its existence at all. "Mittens?" my countrymen wonder aloud. What on Earth would we need mittens for? It's summer! As long as the flowers bloom and it's a hundred degrees in the shade, our collective psyche sits on a patio in a sundress, drinking cold beer, going to the cottage for barbecues, and diving into the lake to cool off.

The short, intense summer is so glorious, it's like the autumn knows that the only way we Canadians could part with summer's long evenings and starry nights is if we are somehow bribed at the time it has to leave us. And in the autumn, every tree and plant seems to be making its apologies to us as though they were guests trying to leave a wonderful, wonderful party. Trees throw massive cloaks of color over their shoulders and let them fall to the ground. Pumpkins arrive in previously ordinary-looking gardens, and everywhere I go there are apples. I do not care very much to eat apples, but it would be impossible to not see the romantic lure of baskets of them piled high in red and green in the autumn. The vegetable shops overflow with the most beautiful of foods; squash and kale and beans are plentiful and inexpensive, and I wander the aisles thinking of making thick vegetable soups and homemade bread.

This time of year the crisp chill returns to the air, and suddenly, after a few short months when we consider wearing wool a one-way ticket to heatstroke, or at the very least an unattractive and linty sweatbath, suddenly it is the most glorious time of year. It's sweater weather.

These slightly frosty days, when there is a nip in the air all day, these are the glory days for knitters. These are the days when people start wishing they had a hat. The evenings when they begin to think about tucking an afghan around them while they watch TV. Yea, verily, these are the days when a woolen throw over the back of a chesterfield stops being ornamental and starts being a pretty smashing idea. These weeks, the weeks before the people reach for their winter coats and conceal their sweaters, these days before the central heat comes on—these are the mighty and triumphant days for a knitter. There will be days in the winter (months, actually, but

I don't like to think about it) when knitting will keep people cozy. There will be snow shoveling and tobogganing, skating, and several blizzards in which the freezing temperatures and blowing snow will demand wool. Days when no one would dream of going outside without a hat and will conduct passionate searches for their mittens, but once it is winter, the knitting will always be in addition to something. They will need their parkas and mittens. Their snowpants and a hat. Your knitted stuff will be useful but will not stand alone. The autumn is a brief interval that is chilly but not freezing, cool but not cold, a few shining weeks when all one needs to cope with the Canadian climate is the fruit of your needles. These days belong to us. These are the weeks when we are most appreciated for what we make and what we do. The few. The chosen. The knitters.

These cool days are also, for many Canadians in general and for my family of McPhees in particular, the beginning of the most esteemed of autumn traditions, the Furnace Wars.

The Furnace Wars are an unspoken and holy contest among our people, a desperate war against nature, trying to delay the inevitable winter by sinking deeply into denial and refusing to give in to the need for central heat. For an intrinsically peace-loving populace, this is really the only serious war we wage, and we lose it every year. It's as if we believe that we can actually shorten our winter by not turning on the heat; that somehow it's not really happening unless you allow it to get the upper hand. (The irony is how cold you have to get to prove that it's not cold, but as with many things to do with pride, not everything about this makes sense.) This time of year, many Canadians obsessively watch the weather forecast and check the thermostat. We say things at the market like "How cold is your house?" or "Did you turn your furnace on yet?," or we boast of our past achievements: "Last year I made it until Halloween." The longer you can go, the colder the house gets, and the less heat you use, the more noble the fight.

As the winter approaches, and we simply must cave in to survive, some of us can't even give up all at once. Last year in the schoolyard I heard a woman say, "I put the furnace on, but only for an hour. I just took the edge off, you know, for the kids. Bob and I can take it."

I know this must seem alien to people who live in areas where winter isn't a long dark challenge to the soul, but here, turning on the heat is like admitting to the beginning of winter, and nobody wants to be the first to cave in. To add fuel to the fire, heat is expensive, both financially and environmentally, and the victors of the Furnace Wars get not just bragging rights but also a low gas bill and a sense of moral superiority. As a knitter, I have other, more compelling reasons to play. This period before I turn on the heat marks the weeks when my art is an important part of the fight. These are the weeks that I look like a genius for making everybody thick wool socks. Everyone wears slippers. They are thinking about full-time indoor hat use. Shawls and throws are over laps and around shoulders. Turning on the heat ends these days of glory for my knitterly self, and that means that central heat is my natural enemy. Unfortunately, this personal sprint for glory is compounded by the fact that I am a member of a very competitive family that enjoys egging each other on in this sort of matter, and I think it gets worse every year.

Last autumn the ongoing battle involved a great deal of confusion. My Uncle Tupper and his wife, Susan, visited my brother Ian for a weekend, and since Susan isn't a McPhee, she compelled him to turn on his heat (if by "compelled" you understand that I mean that she said it was a stupid game). Ian complied (he is nothing if not a good host) and provided heat for the duration of their visit, then turned it off again and outlasted me from that point and tried to claim victory. I say this means he definitely lost, since managing outside influences is part of the Furnace Wars, and why you turned your furnace on is irrelevant. On is on. Ian disagrees, and the lack of clarity surrounding who the victor was has only impelled both of us to greater heights this year, and the game is on.

Ken (my friend and my mother's downstairs tenant) turned on the heat last week, claiming that his roommate was cold (not him, of course) and thus disqualified himself and took my mother out with him. My siblings and I suspected that this might piss off my mother, but it turned out that she had snuck the heat on briefly the week before, and when Ken was accused of ruining it for her, she admitted it. My sister Erin was unceremoniously turfed from the contest three days later when the temperature outside fell to 32°F, and a furtive spy (my daughter, who was babysitting) discovered that she was using her fireplace to heat her home. She defended herself, saying it was the Furnace Wars, not the Heat Wars, but Ian and I discussed it, and we were clear. It's the spirit of the thing that matters. She's out.

Therefore, the two virtuous contestants remaining in the match are Ian and me. In past years I have been held back from the full glory of my skills by the presence of small children, since they get frostbite sooner than adults and can't be dragged into the contest with me, but now they are young women, and the fact that they carry McPhee DNA could not be more apparent. The girls discussed it the other night, and in addition to the financial and environmental rewards reaped by waiting, they also have embraced the glory of kicking their Uncle Ian's arse on this, and I think that even if I wanted to turn on the heat now, I would be outvoted.

Warmed by their allegiance and maturity, I have armed this family with a private weapon. The best defense possible. Knitwear. After all, I am a knitter. I have been arming this family for years with a multitude of sweaters, afghans, socks, arm warmers, fingerless mitts, scarves, and blankets, and now they are about to pay off. Ian, on the other hand, is armed only with determination, spunk, and a couple of pairs of wool socks I made him, although I do see now that the pair of felted slippers I made him were likely a strategic error, and I deeply regret the afghan, but he is my brother, and it was Christmas. I got carried away. I don't think my lapse in tactical warfare will work too far against us, and now that I've wised up about arming my enemy, he's getting a book for his birthday.

Nobody here has asked for the heat yet, although the children did wear layers to dinner last night, but I dropped by Ian's today (I swear it wasn't a furnace spot check). Ian's wife, Alison, was busy putting plastic over all the windows in their house while wearing a hat indoors, which tells me that she might be feeling it. I don't think it's getting to us yet, but last night I did keep falling asleep while I was knitting. I thought I was tired, but now I realize that it's possible that I was slipping into some sort of cryogenic state, and I couldn't really knit with mittens on, which made my fingers a little numb. Still, I thought of the glory and soldiered on, wondering how far it would go this year. These are the Furnace Wars, not the Furnace Amusements, and things could, I thought, go a little too far.

Ian had the same sense (and less knitwear, which may have increased his willingness to negotiate), and we have decided, knowing full well that we both carry the McPhee gene for noncompliance—as well as a Stewart gene for stubbornness and an unreasonable inability to lose anything, anytime, anywhere, to anyone—that if we didn't have a backup plan for when to call this thing quits, someone could get hurt. We've decided that if it snows, or one of us calls the other and broaches a truce, we'll turn on the heat simultaneously and share our status as the family's last stand against winter.

Still, these are my glory days, and as I watch my sixteen-year-old cross the living room in leg warmers, two sweaters, a scarf, hat, and mittens, all the product of my needles, I know the truth. I'm not turning the furnace on until Ian calls me or somebody has to break the ice in the toilet. Put on a sweater.

Tell Me a Story

My whole life, I have been very interested in the potential held in things. I love beginnings, when all is possible and everything could be fantastic and nothing has stepped up to the plate to disappoint me. There is nothing I like more than feeling the weight of a book in my hands and wondering what the story inside might be. I feel an overwhelming excitement at the beginning of movies, and I am sure that this love of pure possibility must be (along with how they smell) one of the reasons I adore newborn babies. I can't wait to see who they might turn out to be.

As I look around my home at all the yarn I jockey around, I'm coming to understand that this love of potential, this urge to see what comes next, it might have something to do with my love for knitting and yarn collecting. After all, yarn is pure potential, and I don't care what anyone says: Knitting is like anything else, you never know how it's going to go. Sure, you can cast on for something with a plan, but there is no guarantee that you're going to end up with it at all. I grant you, sock yarn cast on for socks with a sock pattern beside you usually means you will end up with socks, but even within those tight parameters, I've had lots of times where I really had to wait and see. Will this particular yarn make tight socks? Beautiful socks? How about really comfortable socks that you wear so many days in a row that you hope people can't smell you coming? Maybe, even though it's beautiful yarn and a lovely pattern, the combination will make socks so ugly that to not rip them back would be an insult to feet everywhere. You just don't know. Every yarn, pattern, and knitter begin an adventure when they come together, and each knitting endeavor could result in a triumph, a challenge, or an experience that ends up teaching you something really useful about your work. (Like if you decide to put a lot of beautiful cables around a neckline it won't stretch enough to put your head through, even if you really flatten your hair and hurt your ears, but I digress.)

I have begun knitting projects absolutely sure that I knew what I was making, only to discover that the yarn was seriously opinionated and wasn't hip to my plan. I've had scarves become wraps because the yarn went further than I thought (that was sort of a really skinny wrap, but I make my own rules), and in one particularly surprising event involving my calculations for yardage and the fact that mathematics have always been a deep challenge for me, I set out making a fall jacket and ran out of yarn before I got any more than a chunky wool tank top with one half sleeve. (That one actually turned back into balls of yarn again, since summer wear that gives you heatstroke is of limited use.) I certainly couldn't have predicted that the end result of twenty hours of knitting would land me back squarely at the yarn stage, and if you had told me that it was even a possibility that the project would have gone that way I would have laughed for an hour (and denied it), but like other things that are full of possibility, there you have it.

Another project began with an ordinary yarn being knit into an ordinary cardigan that revealed its magic in the knitting and has ended up being a sweater that is so unordinary that it is my near constant companion. It is one of the best things I've ever made, and I love it so much that I have considered knitting another one just like it as a backup sweater, just in case. I wear it so much that I imagine that someday when my descendants describe me, they will have to mention that sweater, only they will use adjectives like *ratty* and *mothbitten* and wonder why on Earth a knitter didn't have a better one. When I started it, I couldn't ever have predicted that the mundane and inexpensive ingredients I had assembled would end up giving me a sweater that I adore to the point of distraction, but that's exactly what knitting is like. Pure possibility . . . a cosmic crap shoot of possibility.

The intrigue only deepened for me when I realized that knitting success or failure isn't even particularly repeatable or predictable. You can knit one sleeve and have it be exactly the right width, and then repeat the same exact process for the other and end up—for reasons known only to do with fate, gauge, and the fact that you drank one glass of wine during the first sleeve and fought with your spouse during the second—with two sleeves that don't have enough in common to belong on one garment. Add in yarn errors, like the time that you bought ten balls of yarn in the same dye lot, only to discover (when the sweater was finished, of course) that one ball was actually lighter and is now a rather obvious stripe across your belly or breasts, depending on which one you had seriously hoped to downplay. (The knitting fates concerned with the matters of possibility do think it's seriously funny to make your worst feature the only thing people will see coming.)

Don't forget to think about pattern errors or quirks, where the designer, tragically human, doesn't write the neck decreases the same way on both sides (even though human necks are the same way on both sides), and the ability to predict knitting outcomes is starting to be really risky and full of promise for entertainment. If you still feel like knitting isn't an exercise in adventure, mystery, and intrigue that is impossible to predict, finish the whole risk assessment with your own personal potential for error and gift for screwing things up, since only you can be blamed if you knit two left fronts to a cardigan, forget to increase for the arms, or miss three charts on a shawl.

A bag of yarn with your intention to knit it is a wonderful sort of a gamble. The path a knitting project takes on its way to completion isn't usually any less intriguing than a good book (or as tedious as a bad one), and I know that I've been a much happier knitter since I embraced that and stopped trying to be in charge of every yarn's plot. This part, the way that every knitted thing is going to tell me a story, is exactly the something that I think non-knitters are missing when they come into my house, look around at all the yarn, and ask me what the hell I need it for. Some of us, those who have more yarn than they could ever knit in a lifetime, even though we may be very honest people, we tell a lie then. We say, "It's for knitting," and we do our level best to look at the quizmaster as if it's totally reasonable. It took me years of watching the look on their faces at that moment to realize that this is why they think I'm nuts. They aren't stupid. (Or most of them aren't stupid. I shouldn't generalize.) They see all that yarn, they see how fast I'm knitting it up, and then they do a little simple math. This much yarn divided by knitting that fast, why, my goodness, it equals a slice of crazy pie, and in that moment they see that I'm clearly delusional if I think I'm going to make a dent in it. (As an aside, this is entirely the wrong moment to reveal that you're still buying.) After years of reflection and damage to my reputation (and years that I am certain my neighbors have been discussing it), I've decided that I might do a lot better if I tried to explain that its charm doesn't really lie in the knitting.

The yarn in the house, all of it, is not for knitting, although I sure thought that's what it was for when I bought this much of it. It turns out that it's for inspiration, for insight—for the inherently fascinating possibility of what it might become. It is there like a collection of books in a house. It is there for the moment, someday, when I pick some of it off the shelf (or closet, or freezer, whatever) and I cast on, and the whole thing starts. The yarn and I will embark on a thing, even if it's a little thing, and the knitting will start to tell me a story.

As a general rule, once someone knows how I am with all the knitting, they ask me how many projects I have in progress at once.

Occasionally this person is an interested or slightly confused non-knitter, one who can't imagine why you would possibly be knitting more than one thing, but more often it is another knitter, come to scope me out.

Maybe it's a virtuous knitter with only one or two things on the needles, or maybe it's a knitter desperately looking for someone who has more on the go than he does, but either way, they have noticed a parade of things on my needles and begun to suspect that I lack a certain monogamous instinct in the project department. In the past I have skirted this question with various dodgy answers, since I have always suspected that it is a trap. If I answer, no matter what I answer—that I have a few or that I have many—the asker always seems to get a huge "Ah-ha! You are exactly as insane as I have always suspected" expression, or worse, they actually say so out loud before looking rather superior.

This question gets asked in a lot of ways, sometimes boldly, sometimes quietly, sometimes in a private moment between two knitters, but always in a manner that tells you that they are going to decide something about you, something defining the moment you give them the answer. It is not hard to spot the trap, which makes it embarrassing that I still sometimes fall for it. Knitters ask each other "How many?" the way that non-knitters ask each other questions like "What sort of car do you drive?" or "Do you dance?" or the way that women ask men "Boxers or briefs?" with a suspicious raise of the eyebrow. Like asking a date whether he or she likes to dance, knitters ask this question because they believe the answer will reveal something about the kind of knitter (and therefore person) that I am. Mostly, we think that knitters who have just one or two projects on the go are steadfast, dedicated, loyal, and get a lot done, and we suspect that knitters who have many (many) things on the needles are weak willed, inconstant, easily swayed, or even flighty. As a knitter with several projects on the go (and by several I mean "more than you are expecting," no matter how many you are expecting), I would like to take a moment to defend my type. We knitters with mountains of knits in progress are more effective and loyal than you think we are.

See, no matter what anyone suspects about my fealty and its relationship to the number of projects scattered around my house, I do not have this many things on the needles because I am weak willed and pathetically susceptible to wool fumes. (Well, I am weak and pathetically susceptible to wool fumes, but that isn't how I got into this situation. That was the problem in the yarn store and why I bought it, not why I have since cast it all on.)

The problem is that I and many other knitters like me are the exact opposite of what you think we are. We are so effective, so practical, and so dedicated that we enjoy having something to knit with us at all times, no matter what our circumstances. Once you look at it that way, as a sincere sort of loyalty, there is no denying that if you are going to knit everywhere, all the time, not every project is going to be appropriate for every situation. This means that I, or other knitters who have embraced this as a lifestyle, require a rather large assortment of different projects available to us in order to meet this goal. It's all about balance and planning.

Nobody can knit lace in the dark at the movies. (Sorry. I shouldn't say "nobody." I'm sure there are a few crazywild talented knitters out there who are churning out Orenburg lace in the pitch dark at the cinema because they have memorized the chart and can feel the stitches and have the sort of memory that allows them to follow what George Clooney is doing without looking at what their fingers are doing, but I am not one of them, and frankly I think that if you are, you should be at the United Nations sorting out that world peace thing with your huge brain.) I need a simple knit. No shaping, no yarn overs, no stitch or row counting; it needs to be a project that just has plain knitting with nothing happening. It needs to be small so I can tuck it into my purse, and discrete enough that turning it on my lap is not a large and distracting movement for the other moviegoers. (See? I've really given this some thought.) I have solved this dilemma with socks. Assuming that I have finished the ribbing (I can't see what's a knit and a purl in the dark, and if Brad Pitt jumps off that building there's no way I'll be able to remember what I was doing) and that I am not yet at the heel (I can't short row in the dark; it's unreliable), then the straight bits of the leg and feet are perfect for the movies. Round and round, knit every stitch. Perfect.

Other times, I'm looking for something more complicated but not so fussy that I have to use a chart or pattern to any great degree. I want something I can pick up and put down while I work on other things. Five minutes while I'm on hold, ten minutes in the line at the bank, fifteen minutes in a waiting room, or an hour waiting for one of the kids at a lesson or swim meet. No chart holds up well for this sort of in-and-out-of-your-purse action, and the project must be retired from public rotation as soon as it gets too big for easy transport. (There was a lesson learned on a public bus some years ago involving a stranger, an afghan, and my belief that he stole a ball of yarn from me, but that story does nothing for my reputation and I'm not repeating it. No big projects on buses.)

With this, we haven't even scratched the surface of my knit needs. I need a project for the evenings when I'm watching TV. That can be something big and unwieldy that doesn't get moved around much, or I could even choose something more complex, since I'll have the light to read a chart. Charts are fine as long as it's a drama. If it's an action show where you actually need to watch to know what's happening, the chart's back out. (I've learned that if you're "watching" action while knitting, a very great deal of the plot can still be followed if you just listen to the explosions.) Subtitles are their own genre, since chart reading is out if film reading is in. Listening to the radio, I can work on whatever I like, and it would be a shame not to take advantage of the chance to knit something complex with a chart and fussy instructions. After all, my eyes aren't doing anything.

Following these guidelines, I've very efficiently begun a whole lot of projects (plus a few more, because all that simple stuff isn't so simple until it's cast on and counted), and I've placed them in helpful locations. Sock in my purse, hat by the door, simple sweater in a knitting bag by my coat. Mittens on the coffee table, Fair Isle by the chair in the kitchen, top-down cardigan on the dresser by my bed. A scarf is at the top of the stairs, in case I need a backup, and there's another in a basket in the dining room in case I get bored with the first one. In the interest of honesty, I can tell you that there are several things that I started to meet the needs of the moment, but they don't count because I'm ignoring them right now. They are in the hall closet, where they don't try to make eye contact. Just to be sure that I am thoroughly prepared for all contingencies, I've also got several balls of sock yarn with the needles stuck in them, just in case I need to grab four or five in an emergency.

Yessiree, I'm prepared. Totally prepared. Efficient, practical, dedicated, and almost entirely prepared for all knitting contingencies. I'm not in over my head. I am not weak. I am simply extraordinarily well-rounded in the knitting department and prepared to cast on enough projects to prove it. It's not a failing. It's not a lack of commitment. It's being properly committed and prepared to knit at any moment. I know it looks bad, though. I know it looks like a bit of a mess, but really?

It's all about balance and understanding, about loyalty and how many relationships you might need to be really monogamous, in a larger sense.

I'm really good at it. (In a larger sense.)

Knit Two Together

Stories of Belonging, Joining, and Love (Sort Of)

CHAPTER 2

Cass

When I decided to write about how Cass knits, I had in mind that I wanted to talk about how impressive I find her because she lives alone. I don't live alone, I have never lived alone, and I'm not sure what would happen if I lived alone. I harbor a suspicion that I am tidy (inasmuch as I am tidy), organized (same thing), and behaving properly (going to work) only because I have other people living around me who would hold me accountable or phone someone if I gave in to my natural urges to drink nothing but coffee and wine, eat nothing but chocolate and wasabi peas, and do nothing but sit around knitting in my underpants while watching old movies. Cass has nobody to supervise her, and she still tidies her house, goes to work, pays her bills, and knits only when her responsibilities are met. (Sort of.) I wanted to write about that because I am just so keen to understand what the difference is between her and me—why I think I would go feral and start building yarn castles in the kitchen if you let me, and why Cass doesn't. I thought that's what I was going to write about, and while I waited for her to e-mail me the little digital movie of her knitting (she lives in New Jersey and I in Toronto), that's exactly what I thought this would be about. I waited while we tried to sort out the technical challenges of that sort of thing, and by the time a file arrived that worked, that I could open, and that actually had Cass knitting on it, I was so damned happy to see it that I watched it four times before I saw the surprising thing about the way she knits, and I changed my mind entirely.

Cassandra was working on a stockinette swatch, one row knit and the next purl, and I watched carefully as she knit a row. I paused the film, made a series of notes about what I was seeing, and then played the next section. On my little screen, as I peered intently and watched my faraway friend start her next row, I saw her do something stunning. As she made the switch from knitting to purling, she changed everything. Her whole hand position changed. It wasn't a small adjustment she made to accommodate purling; it was a whole other knitting style. There wasn't anything she hadn't changed. She had been palm down, now she was palm up. She held the needle a different way; she even shifted which finger was tensioning the yarn. It wasn't related to what she'd been doing before at all. If I couldn't still see her face, I wouldn't have believed it was still her. I reached for the phone. I called long distance. When she answered I told her that I'd been watching knitters for a long time, and I'd never seen anything as crazy as that. I quizzed her for a while and sort of freaked her out. How the hell did she work ribbing, or any other row where knit and purl both existed. Did she have to change her whole hand position in between every knit and purl? What the hell was her plan? What was she thinking? Cass considered this odd phone call for a minute, and then she said something I've probably heard her say a thousand different times. "What makes you think I know what I'm doing?" she said. "I make changes. I shift things around. I just make it work. Loosen up."

I practically had to put my head between my knees while she was talking. That happens sometimes when I talk to Cass. I'm not a flexible person. I am a creature of habit and routine, and things or people that break up my system or have no system upset me. I am a nervous overthinker, and I tend to stick with what I know, and that means I never say, "I just make it work." I do make things work, I really do, but things working out for me is the direct result (I think) of planning, an attempt at organization, an agonizing amount of contemplation, and a striking relationship with lists and an over-developed fondness for office supplies. Even the way I knit is the result of a carefully contrived efficiency developed over thirty-five years. This idea, what Cass was saying, that she had no idea what she was doing or how, but was doing it anyway, was entirely alien to me. She might just as well have been offering me information in Swahili, and I had to hit the reset button on my psyche and remember again why Cass is in my life. At the risk of sounding like the sort of person who makes her own granola (which I do, but that's not the point), I believe that everyone is here for a reason, that every person has a purpose, and that as itchy as it makes me sometimes, I know why I love Cassandra in my life.

Cass's slogan could be "Evolve or die." She changes whatever she has to, whenever she has to, and I stare at her in wonder. I am bad with change to the point that I could spend a year contemplating switching breakfast cereals and might still feel nervous about my choice. Although she was educated in private schools, studied the liberal arts abroad, and can tell me that my latest writing is "structurally laborious" (and be right), Cass is the sort of person who, when her father died unexpectedly, inherited a business that manufactures (of all things) prison phones, and she didn't miss a beat. I would have been sobbing under a bed somewhere at the thought of taking my extensive knowledge of English romantic literature and my grand plan for my life and flushing it down the toilet, and all Cass did was say, "I don't know how I'll do it, but I will." I'm not going to pretend for a minute that what happened next was easy or pretty, or that Cassandra shifts huge things painlessly, but she took a big hit to her life and her plan, and instead of railing against what needed to happen, she changed. Where someone else might have been paralyzed, a few years later, Cassandra had a whole new life. She had moved to New Jersey, taken up knitting with a passion, found a passel of new friends as a result, and packed a little house right full of yarn before she woke up one bright and shining day and discovered that she had suddenly become the sort of woman who was at a conference in Texas talking to wardens about penal communication systems with expertise and confidence. "I can't believe this is where I am," she said. I think she was surprised that so much had changed, but she might have found it just as unbelievable that it was Texas.

I don't, for the life of me, know why Cassandra can't believe it. The way she knits sums her up. Cass is changeable without being flighty, adaptable without being reckless; she can devise a new approach in a heartbeat if she has to, and she does it all without losing track of her central self. Cass changes her breakfast cereal all the time, and she doesn't even consider it a risk. I love, I am enchanted by, the way that she perpetually does what it takes and is ever moving forward but doesn't have any idea at all that she's doing it. In fact, Cass often thinks she's stuck, both physically and spiritually.

I have never, ever understood how she can feel this way when she's practically the poster child for spiritual growth and remarkable adaptability. I don't know how the sort of person who learns something new every ten minutes and has to tell me to loosen up every fifteen can think of herself as stuck, but I have wondered whether Cass gets this message because her life doesn't have very many of the traditional markers and milestones that we use to manage the progress of a woman's life. She's single, she has no kids, and she owns her own business, so it's not even like she gets promoted for learning or doing a good job. In my life, I get clues that there is movement. I have a career where success is measured in one project coming after the other, my kids get older and more accomplished, and my relationship with my husband matures, even if that only means that I finally understand that he's never going to be on time for anything. I couldn't possibly feel stuck; there's movement showing me the flow of my progress all around me. Cass gets up every day and the backbone of her life stays the same, and I think that can make her think she's in a loop and not on a journey.

All of this has turned out to be tremendously ironic, because when Cass stomped into my life at a thousand miles an hour, I thought I was moving forward, and she thought that she was going nowhere, both of us tricked by the things around us. I had very good friends, and I wasn't, when Cass turned up, in the market for more. I am the sort of person who forms good and long friendships, and the friends I had at the time were all the same friends I had enjoyed for decades. They were very good friends, and they still are, but I believed, because I had not had a new friend in so long, I believed that I had been given my lifetime allotment of them, and like eating the same cereal every day, that didn't bother me at all.

Enter Cass, who broke the seal on all my beliefs about friendship with her flexibility, changeability, and knack for adaptation. Her ability to do whatever worked was a challenge to my system (my system being to keep doing whatever I was doing, whether it was working or not), and this same flexibility has turned out to be the best foil for my nervous nature. I tend to come reluctantly (if by *reluctant* you understand that I resist it as cats resist bathing) to new things, even good things, and Cass found ways to convince me that new things and new people could fit into my life, if only I would loosen up, follow where she was leading, and see that change could look good on a person. Only someone as flexible (and persistent) as Cass could have possibly unlocked someone as rigid as I was, and her arrival and consequent bashing down of my internal door marked the beginning of what I now think of as the second wave, a group of women that I simply cannot do without, that Cass brought me at this unexpected time in my life, when I really thought I had a system and all the friends I was going to get.

When I think about my natural reticence about new things or new people and how it almost held me back from discovering this wonderful friendship; when I think about all the other people the goddess Cassandra dragged into my life with me twitching and screaming; when I look at her knitting like that, switching whole systems to get from knit to purl, I know why she's here. Cass has taught me a thing or two about there being more than one way to solve a problem, more than one way to look at things, and that if you knit your way across a row, you haven't made a permanent decision about how you have to hold your hands when you purl back. Without Cass, I wouldn't be anywhere near where I am today, and I have no idea at all how I made it this far without her. She is a walking testament to flexibility and movement in a human, and everything about her has taught me a lot about opening myself up to possibility, friendship, and the things that knitting and people can bring you, if only you can be flexible enough to see the potential. She's shown me, in short, which one of us was stuck, and that there is more than one way for a woman to measure her success.

I may also change my breakfast cereal. Maybe.

A List of People Who Are Not Getting a Knitted Gift from Me and the Reasons Why

(I know that's sort of a long title, but I think it is justified. Something must be done.)

1. My aunt Christine. Removed from the list for telling me that the scarf that I knit her looked "almost as good" as the one that my cousin got her from Wal-Mart. It was all I could do to contain myself. Seriously. What sort of world are we living in where one woman could spend hours and hours and hours of her time making something, by hand for another human, essentially creating something out of hours of her own life, and someone could think that it's okay to compare the result of those hours of human effort to a stinking machine-knit commercial thing from an uberconglomerate with no soul? Seriously. No knits for you.

2. My husband, Joe. For not trimming his toenails to a length that I feel is safe for handknit socks. I am tired of the argu-

ment that the holes that develop right over his big toenails are a coincidence or a consequence of his shoes. It happens in boots, it happens in shoes, it happens in sneakers, and it happens when he is shoeless. Dude, it is your toenails. Kindly cut them to a length I consider secure for handknit socks, or I'm pulling your supply. (Okay. I'm not pulling the supply. I am thinking about being a little slow with the next pair, though. Better watch your step.)

3. My friend Ken, for telling me that the last pair of socks I knit him were "too purple" and perhaps "not manly" or "for real men." The last time I checked, my notorious friend, you were lucky to be getting handknit socks at all, and what you should be feeling, my good buddy, even if your socks are pink and frilly with big honking ruffles over the heels, is nothing but gratitude that I have been so good as to knit you a pair. Too purple indeed. Real men suck it up. The next lace pair I make are going to be in your size.

4. That lady on the bus who explained to her friend that knitting was simple and fast and took hardly a minute. I've got nothing against you, lady, but there's no way I'm ever knitting you something if you think that all this stuff falls off me while I'm walking. No way.

5. My ex-boyfriend Stewart from the eleventh grade. He knows why.

6. The baby next door who doubled his birthweight in forty-five days and had the audacity to outgrow the sweater I made him, having only worn it once. (He is not off the list permanently— just until he stops growing faster than I can knit or his parents

stop feeding him so well.)

7. My cat, since there is a stunning felted cat bed I made her that she hasn't even looked at. I have discovered that it is important to my happiness that I do not knit for beings that do not say thank you, may not use what I knit at all, and may not even admit that the beautifully knitted gift is in the room with them. Now that I think about it, there's a cousin I'm taking off the list for the same reasons.

8. Anyone, ever, who has, when I asked them if they would like a hand knit, replied with "Ummm."

9. Anyone with a foot size greater than men's 13, or a chest (of either gender) that measures more than 52 inches. I want to be able to continue to like you when I'm done knitting for you and not hold you in contempt for your size and its attendant effect on my sanity. (Or lack thereof.) Would you like a scarf?

10. Margaret, or so her name tag read, an employee of my local grocery store who, noticing me knitting as I stood in the exceedingly long line for the checkout, said to the employee she was walking with, "Wow. How lame does your life have to get before you're reduced to knitting at the grocery store?" She does not respect the Knit-Force, and knits will not be bestowed upon her. I hope she's chilly.

All Knitters

I have an obsession. Beyond being rather unnaturally interested in knitting as a whole, knitters in general, and yarn in specific, I am absolutely captivated by the actual act of knitting. Not knitting as it turns out sweaters and hats and socks, but the movements that make up the act of knitting. How a knitter's fingers go, what a knitter's hands do . . . where and how they hold the yarn. I haven't always cared about this or watched knitters knit, and I know that if you've never done it, really watched them, this little interest of mine probably sounds a little as if my other hobbies might be watching paint dry or grass grow. It began when I tried to learn to knit another way. I wanted to be able to do two-color knitting with two hands, and since I've always carried the yarn only in my right hand, my left hand needed to be taught a lesson. I sat down to work it out, and I sat down with confidence.

At the time I had been knitting "my way" for more than twenty years. I cannot even begin to guess how many stitches I had knit, but it had to be millions. I was sure that there would be a learning curve on this, but I'm proud of my skills as a knitter, and I'm a fast learner. Well, pride goes before a fall, let me tell you. The minute I put the yarn in my left hand the whole thing fell apart. Not just apart where you carry the yarn, either; the entire system came apart. Every knitting skill I had ever had just dissolved. The yarn slipped off my finger no matter how I tried to tension it; I dropped needles. I knew what had to happen, I knew what went where, but it was like I couldn't get a message to my hands. Within a few minutes I was incompetent and tangled, and since patience isn't really my forte, I got more and more frustrated. I am used to being ungainly and inept when I'm doing almost anything else, but knitting is not an area of my life where I'm used to feeling like I can't manage. Knitting is what I do to reassure myself that I'm not an absolutely inadequate moron, and I don't have a lot of coping skills for abject knitting failure. I started to curse and behave sort of badly, and then, in a moment that I admit was not the pinnacle of my maturity and I'd rather my children had not witnessed, I threw the knitting (or lack of it) on the floor and stomped off. (It is only because I feared puncture that I did not stomp on the knitting itself.)

Badly unsettled, I took a couple of turns around the house and then sat down to knit . . . my way. Maybe I was missing something. I took up the needles and twined the yarn around my fingers, and I felt everything settle into its familiar place. I began to effortlessly make stitches, one after another, and I boggled. How could I go from this string of perfect stitches to mere moments later acting like I'd never held a set of needles, just by changing one simple thing? I looked down at my hands as they knit, trying to figure out what I was missing. I watched myself make a stitch, watched it slip from one needle to another. I watched the whole thing, and as I watched, I realized something. Knitting wasn't simple. Well, knitting was simple. Knitting was just pulling one loop through another using a stick. Knitting was the simplest thing in the world; it's how I was doing it that wasn't simple.

If I just quickly looked at my hands, it looked like my left hand was still, just holding the needle, and that my right hand moved its needle into the stitch, flicked forward to wrap the yarn, then pulled back and took the finished stitch off the left needle. Three steps. In, around, off. In, around, off. That's all I was trying to replicate. In, around, off. Any idiot could do it, and that's when I noticed something.

My left index finger. I thought that I had just been holding the needle between that finger and my thumb, but suddenly I became aware that my finger was doing something. As I began each stitch, that finger subtly moved the stitch along the needle to the tip, holding it for the right needle and separating it from its peers. I stared at my hand. This explained a lot. When I tried to reverse my knitting and learn a new way to do things, I hadn't even thought about this. I had no finger doing this job. I was just doing "in, around, off." I stared at my finger. How incredible that this finger had this whole vital knitting job that I didn't even know existed. Here I am, having knit a hundred million stitches over decades of experience, and I didn't even know that finger was vital. No idea. I knit another

I took to watching people while they knit. (I tried to be discreet. I may not always have been successful.) I began to investigate theories. What did the way you knit say about you? Do you knit the way you do because of personality traits? Physical traits? Were people who were tight knitters wound tightly themselves? Were loose knitters relaxed? I looked at the body posture of knitters, the way the needles sat in their hands, the way that they wrapped the yarn around the needles, and as I watched, an enormous thing began to reveal itself. No two knitters knit the same way. Even knitters who on the surface appeared to have identical styles—both holding the needles the same way, both carrying the yarn in their left hands, both wrapping the yarn with the same movement—on examination they were worlds apart. One would lean forward over her work with rapt attention, the other would lean back in her chair. One would push stitches along with an extra finger, the other would move stitches with the needle, resting her finger along the back of her work. Alice was quick; Margaret made large swoops with her throwing hand; Hannah scooped up the yarn in a tiny, efficient movement; Genevieve kept her work close to her because she doesn't like to wear her glasses, but Jane holds it farther away because she has an ample "front porch." Ken has no such barrier. They were all unique, their own style grown up from who they are and what they've learned and how their own stuff works.

I have been watching knitters semiprofessionally for years now, and I have yet to find any two who knit in a way that is absolutely identical, and that's pretty staggering, because when you think about it they are all getting exactly the same product. All of them. If I asked fifty knitters to knit me a square of garter stitch, knit at five stitches to the inch, I would get fifty very identical squares. I would never in a million years be able to see the degree of personality that went into making them. I know that I probably wouldn't even be able to pick my own out of the pile. In the absence of a very personal error or two, they would all be indistinguishable and identical, and that makes me so happy that I almost laugh out loud.

Think about it. People have been knitting on Earth for, at our best guess, about a thousand years. I won't even begin to try and calculate how many knitters that means there have been, but know that at present there are about 50 million people who know how to knit in North America alone, and we're less than 10% of the world's population. Think that over, add in the rest of the world (remember, China is superbig, and knitting is superbig in China), multiply it by that thousand years, and wonder how many tens of thousands of millions of knitters have all held the needles the way you do today, only nothing like you do. Every single one of them, all knitting. All knitters use needles, all knitters use yarn. All knitters wrap the yarn around the needles and pull a new loop through, all knitters, all millions and millions and millions of them, making billions and billions of stitches that all look exactly the same when they are done, and not one of them, out of all that human history, not a single soul is doing it exactly the way that you do.

I know this, because I've been looking. You should, too.

Ten Ways to Make a Knitter Love You More

1. Call your modest collection of handknit socks your "real" socks.
2. Offer to drive any time you're in a car together.
3. While you're driving, offer to stop by the yarn store, just for fun.
4. Say, "Man, I love the smell of wet wool in the morning" and really mean it.
5. Develop a fetish for handwashing things.
6. Get a T-shirt that says "Moth Hunter."
7. Claim that you love how cozy your home looks with all this wool in it.
8. Tell your knitter that you think knitting charts are not just clever but dead sexy.
9. On Valentine's Day, know that red sock yarn is cheaper than roses and lasts a lot longer.
10. Knit, but only a little, and with your own damn yarn.

Love Letter

Sitting here, nestled in your warm embrace, I realize that you have come into my life to complete me. There have been so many times in the past when love didn't work out for me, that I almost forgot that it was possible to feel like this, to know real, perfect love. I've suddenly learned that we can look forward in our futures and try to exert control over the way thing go, and spend so much time planning how we will get the things we want, but the truth is that some relationships either work out or they don't, and a lot of that is destiny, far beyond what I can predict.

Knowing you and the warmth you've brought to my life has also proven to me that when things work out, it isn't only destiny, because the relationship has had enough work put into it that the fit has gotten to be just right. You can't let the thing get so big that it consumes everything you've got and smothers your own self, but neither can you allow it to become constricting, limiting, and small, becoming a thing that makes you feel like you're the wrong size yourself. For so many years of my life I have worked to get something just like this. Opening myself and everything that I had to the possibility, trying to get rid of the old patterns I kept falling into, and hoping that this time, when I began a new relationship, it would work out, even though there have been so many disappointments. I knew I had what it would take to make this happen, but over and over I have been so hurt when it didn't turn out to be what I thought it would be.

It's terrible to think of, now that I have these days with you, coming out on the other side of all those times the magic didn't happen, times when I found that something that had seemed so right turned out to be harsh or too difficult, times when I made mistakes and endured injustices that were such an insult to my soul that I was almost afraid to try again. I was so frightened of the cost and wasted time that I had trouble even imagining a relationship that could end up being this deep—rich love that goes so far past a simple infatuation.

None of this is to say that what we have was easy to get. Heaven knows we've had our difficulties getting here. I know that you were as frightened as I was a few months ago, when it seemed like everything was coming undone. Loving you has taught me that sometimes you have to take calculated risks, to gauge what is possible. To extend trust to the process that has brought this into being. When I first saw you, I could only guess at what it could all become; you seemed so strong and sturdy, I wouldn't have ever guessed that you had such a soft side.

I may be a hopeless romantic, but I am old enough not to be naive. I know how seldom this perfect a love comes into anyone's life and how lucky I am that it worked out for us. I know, too, that time will pass, and we may someday be parted. Nothing can last forever, and that only makes you more of a treasure to me. You have taught me not to give up. You have taught me to open myself up to the wonder of a relationship that makes me feel so complete and safe when you wrap yourself around me.

Until I met you and learned that I could learn to do this, realized that I wasn't going to be left out of something I saw other people finding, there was an empty place I didn't know I had. Until I met you, I was a little cold.

You are really the best sweater I've ever had.

Love,
Stephanie

P.S.: Don't take the new pullover on the needles too personally. I have enough room in my heart for two.

CHAPTER 3

Yarn Over

Stories of Challenging People,
Projects, and Knitters

Denny

My friend Denny is knitting. I love, with a helpless and unreasonable passion, the way she knits. I just love it. The way Denny knits breaks all the rules about knitting I've ever been told or made up for myself. Denny holds her hands, palms down, with her fingers curled loosely under, like for sleep. The needles rest in the curls of her fingers, so relaxed that I am constantly surprised that she doesn't drop them. The yarn she is using, a softly spun alpaca, snakes up from the handwoven basket by her feet and snakes forward along the line of the right needle toward its tip, passing under her palm and through the curve of her fingers. When most people knit, they tension the yarn somehow; we're all told that it's necessary to come up with a system for this, or our work will be uneven or loose. You need to press it between two fingers or wrap it around one of them or do something, but Denny didn't get the memo, and she doesn't do anything at all to control the yarn. It just lies there, unbound and uncontained, under her palms. Her hands rest in her lap, not tense well, I'm still not sure why she was there. She was already perfectly competent at the wheel, the loom—everything to do with fiber was already something she was good at, but somehow, and I hope Denny knows what I mean when I say this, I couldn't tell that.

The teacher was a serious sort, and that was fine with me because I was there to learn. The room contained a few other students, looms of all sorts, spinning wheels of all types, drum carders, hand cards, distaffs, and odd piles of fiber, and sitting there, in the middle of all of this incomprehensible stuff, was Denny. Denny is not supermodel material, which is not to say that she isn't beautiful in a surprising way. She's a little short, average weight, plain brown hair, even her age would be hard to pin down. She's not old, nor young; she's right in the middle, and she'd be hell to describe to a police sketch artist. There's nothing remarkable about her—except, somehow, all of her. She was dressed, as she almost always is, in an outfit that defies description. Denny is one of those people who can wear whatever she wants and look grand. Denny can put on striped tights, a plaid skirt, a handknit sweater in a color that is not present in the stripes or the plaid, top it with a red velvet jacket and a white lace scarf, toss on German shoes, and look inspired. It's a gift. If I put on the same outfit I would look crazy, or homeless, or both. I can spend forty-five minutes picking out my clothes, and I will still look like I grabbed my outfit out of the dryer in the dark, but when Denny wears it, she looks artistic and creative and original. I'm standing in this class, dead serious and a little nervous, and here she comes, wearing I don't know what, laughing, gesturing, making tea (when there was a huge "no food or drink" sign), breaking every rule that there was about everything, and I was taken aback. I didn't know what to do with her. She was much too much for me, and that's saying something, since I'm often accused of the same thing.

She was odd as fish, that lady, and my unease went on for weeks, and for a while there, if I'm being really honest, I can tell you that not only did I distrust Denny because she was an unknown quantity, but I think I actually disliked her for breaking the rules and getting away with it. Actually, not just getting away with it, but making the most of it, rising above it . . . thriving on it. Denny had more individuality in her little finger than I had in my whole body, and I was a little resentful. I wanted to be like that, so firmly me that I didn't let anything stand in my way, and with that thought I caught the magic, and whether I wanted to or not, I started to admire her, and then to like her (quietly, and while she wasn't looking), and then to genuinely love her and take her as a friend.

The magic was this: Denny is so uniquely, profoundly, and unapologetically herself that something crazy happens when you see her. Usually, when you meet someone remarkable like that, you are so awestruck by the wonder that is them that you feel a little bit like you want to be like them. You start to think highly of them, look up to them. And Denny's not like that. You don't look up to Denny, and she wouldn't be capable of looking down on anyone. She looks across at you, and somehow you're inspired by her not to be more like her but to be more like yourself, whatever that is, and I think that's why Denny's best nature breaks all those rules, and it's why she gets away with it.

It's even there in the way she knits. You're not supposed to be able to knit the way Denny does and not suffer the wrath of the knit fates. If you don't use patterns, don't do swatches, don't even tension your yarn, then you're going to have trouble. Her knitting should be terrible. It should look sloppy and uneven and show the lack of rules like the knitter's version of a scarlet letter, but it doesn't, and that drives us all nuts—for a while, and then you start catching on. There's a reason Denny's done away with the rules. She has to be unique and dance to her own drummer and do it all her way, so that you're inspired to start playing around with the rules about who you are.

There are still people who don't catch Denny's magic. People who find her all the things I found her to be before I came to understand why I met her, what her magic is, and why I think she's here. There are people who can't get the hang of it or are offended by all the rule breaking, people who talk about how she doesn't fit in, and I wonder about those people. If Denny's gift is the ability to make you want to be more like yourself, then what about those people who can't get used to her? Maybe they just don't like who they are enough to want to be themselves.

to the status of a role model in the knitting community, and your designs are everywhere waiting to ~~assault~~ delight and enlighten knitters worldwide, and I feel that in exchange for this honor, you have a certain responsibility to us, the humble knitters gathered at your feet. I feel that even though you never answer any of these letters, you must bind each of them to your heart and deeply contemplate all that I write to you.

It is because we have this close (albeit somewhat one-sided) relationship that I was among the many knitters gathered around you at the bookstore where you gave a talk last week, and I was listening carefully to everything you had to say about your work and your calling, and it just so happened that I was sitting right next to the girl who asked you about the difficulties she had encountered with one of your fanciest colorwork sweaters. Her problems involved having so many different colors operating in one row that the number of yarns she had to carry along the rear of her work resembled a rope that would have been entirely at home along the bow of a transatlantic ship, and, I hope you recall, she had asked you for some direction about how she should accomplish this task. Nay, Dear Designer, she had asked what you, the matron of all knitters, the lighthouse by which we guide our yarny journeys, how you yourself managed to carry the seven (or was it eight?) strands of yarn that needed to be transported along that section of Fair Isle knitting.

I leaned forward then, for as you may recall from my fourteen-page letter of last October, I had tried to knit that sweater, and it was that exact row she was talking about that had resulted in the incident

I sent you all of the full-color photos of, and since your answer to me had certainly been lost in the mail I waited to hear what you would say. How had you handled it?

Imagine my shock, imagine how completely stupefied I was, when you looked this woman in the eye, this woman who had (as we all do, I am sure you are aware) put all of her knitterly time and faith (as well as a fair bit of her yarn money, not that we think of the insignificance of mere cash when we are knitting one of your patterns) into working this sweater pattern of yours and supporting your career, and you told her (and this is an exact quote, since this moment is burned into my memory forever) that you "had heard the test knitter say there were some real challenges" but that you had "never actually knit that pattern."

Never knit it? Never? You turned that row with the eight colors (because it was eight, you lunatic, I just went and looked) loose on the world without any sort of warning at all? Furthermore, you (without having strangled six of your ten fingers trying to follow your chart) had the audacity to have the caption beneath the photo read, "This charming summer pop-over, just bursting with the colors of the season, works up quickly thanks to sport-weight yarn and flirty cap sleeves."

Flirty cap sleeves? Works up quickly? Your test knitter (who must be a saint among women; would you mind sharing her address? I'd like to send her a ~~sympathy card~~ box of chocolates) told you that there were "some challenges," you knew full well that you had eight colors in a row in your "flirty cap sleeves," and you still felt that it

was honorable to ~~inflict this on~~ share this with the world without
having tried to knit it yourself?

Now, I am not a naive woman, my dearest designer, and deep in
the seat of my intellect (which surely pales compared to your own)
I was aware that you could not be knitting each and every one of
these patterns. It is impossible for a designer to make a full-time
living out of creating knitwear if they knit every masterpiece themselves. Knitting is too slow for any knitter, even a wonder such as
you, to produce enough patterns in one year that she wouldn't have
to moonlight as a waitress at a local diner for the privilege. That
part of me should not have been surprised. The rest of me sure was,
though, as I sat there in that audience realizing that not only could
you not give this woman, this fellow knitter, any help at all, but you
also could not offer any real sympathy, not even a shred, and I was
suddenly so shocked that I could scarcely breathe, and the world
swirled blackly around me.

When I regained consciousness (having thankfully been caught
by a loop of my circular needle so as not to fall into the aisle; can you
imagine how mortified I would have been if I had disrupted your
talk with the sound of my body hitting the floor?), I had sudden
clarity of thought. As I tried to explain it to you right then (seriously,
does a knitwear designer need "security forces"?), it is not that you
didn't knit these things that stunned me. It was not lying awake
wondering whether you could knit these at all that perplexed me. It
was the realization that you and I are not in the same boat together
after all, that when I knit your patterns it doesn't link my work to

yours in a beautiful chain of continuous art; we don't share high moments and low points together, we are not having a shared experience in the slightest. I can no longer take solace in the idea that if it was possible for you, it must be possible for me.

As my fellow knitters and I await the latest inspired manipulation of wool and genius to fall from your pen and in our general direction . . . perhaps you could do us the humble and profound honor of at least knitting a freaking swatch of the damned thing before you inflict it on us.

It is only fair, Dear Designer, because if we do not stand together as knitters, then we do not stand at all (or sit, actually, because it is less comfortable to knit standing up, but you know what I mean).

Thank you.

Your humble servant,
Stephanie

This Is a Test

I think I am understanding it now. This is a test. A test of my character or my will or something. Some higher power has decided to find out what I'm made of, and lo and behold, my test has come not in the form of a child to be rescued from a burning building or a choking stranger who needs the Heimlich maneuver. Nor has it come in the form I most feared: I took French until I graduated and was congratulated on that day with the knowledge that now that I had completed grade thirteen French, my government considered me bilingual. I feared that my allegedly bilingual nature would be recorded, that my name would be written on some large official list of people who could be counted on to translate French in a pinch, and that all of this would culminate in some incredible nightmare of an afternoon when a desperate police officer pounded on my door and dragged me into the street to perform a French-speaking function to save thousands of lives—something like defusing a French bomb. I have imagined this moment ever since that day, and in this horrible vision I imagine myself horror struck, finally realizing that the moment of testing is upon me, and all I think of in that terrible moment is that my final grade in French was only a 64, and that means I am only 64% bilingual, and it's been years since then so it's probably much, much less, and I try to explain that to the police. I try to tell them they should get someone else, and they just won't listen because my name is on the list, and I do my best but kill us all through my pathetic lack of French, and the last thought that passes through my mind as the bomb explodes is that it all could have been different if I had done just a little more homework. That would be a character test with some drama. That is more in keeping with what I thought the ultimate test of my self would be, but no. The same way I was disappointed to discover that parenthood is really mostly about washing things, it turns out that the test of my character that I have felt was coming for forty years turns out to be a tiny cream baby bonnet.

I have, at the time of this writing, ripped it back out no less than eight times, and I swear to you in the name of everything I hold dear that if I had not promised my sister-in-law that I would work this out (and if I had not been cocky and self-assured when I did so), I would have shoved the whole thing in my mouth by now, gnawing at it until my eyeteeth were sharpened with rage and I could spit sodden bits of it upon the dirty ground until my revenge felt entirely sated. The last time I was this frustrated by something this small it was an eight-pound newborn human who had invested in a personal mission to keep me awake for days on end and then puked on me to make the point. I didn't take action then only because I loved the thing, and it took me thirty-seven hours of labor to get (other than that, I would probably have abandoned it, at least for a little while).

I owed this bonnet no such allegiance.

It had started, as all the best tests of character do, with a pretty ordinary event. (Tests of character are like that. The person who is to be tested seldom has any warning.) My sister-in-law Kelly, who, despite how it went down later, is actually a very nice person who (I think) bears me no malice, showed me a small thing and confessed an obsession. She produced, out of the things her daughters had when they were babies, a wee bonnet. It was cream-colored plain wool. Fine wool, too, the weight called "baby" that always seems so perfect for tiny new beings, and it was a little felted and worn from frequent and affectionate use. It was garter stitch, plain knitting every row, it had a wee peak that dipped down onto the baby's forehead, and it tied under the chin with ivory satin ribbon stitched to the front bottom corners. The hat itself, as much as it was simple and charming, was rather queerly wrought, and this was the challenge. It was knit side to side somehow, with short rows to shape the crown (I thought) and subtle casting on and off to make the peak. Kelly felt in her heart of heart that this hat was the best and possibly only thing that she could knit for an impending baby, but the pattern had been lost. Kelly had received that hat while she was living in Denmark with her babies, and she had been so enchanted with this style of bonnet, so unlike anything she'd ever seen before, that she had asked the knitter for the pattern. She'd received it, not in the form of a book or a leaflet, but handwritten on a piece of paper. Kelly had cherished it for years, this heirloom pattern, but as time passed and they moved from country to country, she had misplaced it. Now she needed it so she could carry on this time-honored tradition and bless a friend's new baby with it. Was there anything I could do to help?

I told Kelly that I would figure it out, and I examined it thoroughly, took careful notes, and began what I thought would be a simple matter of reverse engineering. I'd done it before with vintage knits that had no patterns, and although this looked a little tricky, rescuing this Danish folk pattern from extinction seemed like a worthy endeavor.

The first attempt was half a misshapen blob. I had the sense to abort the mission when it was obvious that I wasn't even in the hat department. The second improved markedly and was a whole, shaped blob. The third one began to resemble a bonnet, although only to me, and I admit I had insider information—I knew I was aiming for a hat. The fourth one was the first attempt that looked like a hat to another person. I asked the kids what they thought it was, and they said, "A bonnet." Well, it wasn't their first guess, but they ran through the possibilities ("Doily? Sleeve? Doll scarf? Booties? Bonnet?"), and it was at least on the list. I realized I had a lot of work to do on it, though, when Amanda chastised Meg for her guess. "Bonnet? Holy cow, Megan, do you even have eyes? It doesn't look anything like a bonnet." Bad sign.

After that fourth attempt, I took a little break. I had been knitting this one demented hat for more than a week, and all I had was the memory of my failures. I felt like I was in *Groundhog Day*, that movie where Bill Murray has to wake up and do the same day of his life over and over and over again until he gets it right. Actually, no. If it was the same day over and over, there wouldn't be more laundry piling up around me while I sat for days on end fiddling with a bonnet. I thought about quitting, but I was the arse who had told Kelly that reverse engineering this hat would be simple, and there was no way I was going to her and admitting that I had failed this test of character. Especially not to Kelly. She really was bilingual. It was very overwhelming.

The fifth hat was a breakthrough. It was actually hat shaped. It wasn't shaped like the hat in question, and I was still having big problems with that peak, but it was so nice to see anything like headgear at all that I thought about buying more wool and having that one bronzed. The sixth one had a peak, but it was totally too long, and instead of dipping fetchingly over the baby's brow, this one would have covered eyes and nose and doubled as a pacifier. Still, it was a peak, and I was so thrilled and relieved about it that I thought about calling Kelly and telling her that I was getting closer. Then I decided I would rather the thing looked effortless. There was no reason anyone needed to know about any of this. They certainly didn't need to know that I had developed an odd habit of chewing on my lower lip every time I saw baby wool, that the kitchen floor was so dirty that I was starting to worry that the cat would get stuck down to it, and that when I thought about it, I wasn't sure I had seen my youngest child in a few days.

The seventh one was a wonder to behold. It was exactly right. I

had at that moment, thinking up revenge strategies against the wool, was hardly going to be productive. Whoever came up with this little hat in the first place clearly had more mental resources than I did, especially since I'd taken to drinking in the afternoon since about hat four. I needed help if I was going to pass this test of character.

I dragged myself upstairs to my pattern library. I have half a million knitting books, magazines, and leaflets; one of them I thought, has to have some help in it. I began thumbing through them, making piles around me, sitting on the floor. I hadn't brushed my hair in a while. I had little wisps of cream baby wool stuck to my pants. By the time I'd pulled about half the magazines and books off the shelves hoping for even a shred of inspiration, I had developed a tremor in my right hand that was probably caffeine withdrawal, and not even the cat would make eye contact with me. I toyed with the idea of "good enough" and imagined the moment that I showed my reverse-engineered heirloom baby hat to Kelly and gave her the pattern that was almost right. I imagined her dejection, and then I picked up another book. I'm not good at much, but I could be good at this.

As nighttime came, I was beginning to lose hope. I'd been through all the magazines and read all the articles with promising titles, and I'd started to feel as if the only solution to this was going to be changing my name to Lola, moving to San Francisco, and taking up papier-mâché to erase all shreds of my previous identity. (I probably would have felt less strongly about that in the morning.) I pulled another book off the shelf and started flipping through it. On page 38, I stopped, and suddenly I could hear the blood pounding in my head. My heart was beating irregularly, I'm sure of it—and if there was ever a time that you could apply the word "ashen" to someone's complexion, I feel it was mine. The air rushed out of my lungs in horror.

The pattern for the heirloom hat, the old pattern passed on by Danish grandmothers for generations, wrought by memory and intuition on the needles of a Danish knitter and passed on to Kelly on a scrap of yellowed paper, long lost now, this charming expression of Scandinavian history and style that I had been trying to reverse engineer for more than a week in order to provide Kelly with a way to carry on the tradition in her own life so that this pattern didn't die out and be lost to all of humanity . . .

It was on page 38 of an American knitting book. It wasn't old at all. It wasn't historic at all. The knitter that Kelly knew in Denmark must have written it out from the book when Kelly asked for it, and Kelly had inferred the rest. I stared and stared. If the roof of my house had caved in at that moment I would have done nothing to save myself. I just would have sat there, the full pattern, clear as day, laid out in front of me.

It had truly been a test of my character. That was the only possibility, and I couldn't even tell whether I'd passed or failed. Damn, I thought, looking at the pattern. At least it wasn't in French.

Mother Says . . .

Parenting is a really odd racket. It encourages a human being to become flexible, quick thinking, strong, and resilient, even under the worst or most challenging circumstances. (We will pause now and silently reflect that this is also the goal of the Navy SEALs.) Each moment could bring utter delight, a test of your patience, or an engulfing house fire.

In exchange for stretching the absolute limits of human endurance by depriving you of sleep, cash, and warm meals, there are no performance appraisals and no corporate board to take the human rights violations to. I don't know how other people do it, but I personally have managed to survive parenting by accepting each moment for what it is. A tiny slice of life. A little jewel of human experience. Potential for a court case or the reason that my kids will someday say that they are in therapy. When I am an older woman, my children will be grown, and I will lead a boring, simple life filled with things like novels, clean pants, uninterrupted knitting time, and long soaks in the tub. I'm sure when that day comes, days like this one will seem almost sweetly sentimental in my recollection.

In thinking of that, I have decided to take a few moments to put down my knitting and write a few of the things that I have found myself saying out loud over the years.

- I don't know if skunks are vegetarians. Wait, are you going outside? Why do you need to know what skunks eat?
- Cats don't eat coffee beans. (Correction for the sake of accuracy: It appears that *most* cats don't eat coffee beans.)
- Where is the toilet paper? (I know this doesn't seem significant, but when you have ten rolls in the morning and none at dinner, it bears a little investigation. They were eventually discovered hidden and unraveled in various locations. Six rolls were salvageable.)
- Yes, I'm sure that blocks won't go down the toilet. (Every well-trained mother knows that all toilet questions should be followed by immediately arming yourself with a plunger and proceeding to the nearest bathroom.)
- Where is my pen? (I once took a message by writing on my arm with mascara. It was neither my message nor my mascara.)
- Because Barney is stupid, that's why.
- Because it can kill you. (Why they can't live without grown-ups.)
- Stop looking at your sister.

- Do you still have two eyebrows? (Eyebrow plucking on a fourteen-year-old never ends well. Don't hope for anything but disaster.)
- Hey! Birds can't do that!
- You need a job.
- What happened to your hair? (Repeat after me: "It's not my hair, it's not my hair, it's not my hair." If you still feel upset, repeat, "Hair grows back, hair grows back, hair grows back.")
- Because it can kill her. (Why they can't lower their sister down the railing of the stairs using my yarn as a rappelling rope.)
- Why do you sound like money?
- Because I think knitting is relaxing, not stupid.
- I told you not to look at her.
- Where would I get three fluorescent light bulbs and a length of hose at midnight? (I hate science fairs.)
- He's a teenage boy. We all know what he's thinking.
- Because it can kill you. (Why you can't play hide-and-seek with the dryer as your hiding place.)
- I can't make a bike bigger with the power of my mind! (This really did seem like the only appropriate answer. I have never been given a reasonable explanation for what my children think I'm going to be able to do about an outgrown bike at 10:12 on a Sunday night.)
- Why is this so sticky? (Lemonade concentrate is not paint.)
- Just because I'm not here doesn't mean I can't see you! (Okay, so I was coming a little undone.)

- I don't care what Linda says. Thunder is not God bowling.
- Because it can kill you. (Why drying your hair while you are in the bath doesn't save people time.)
- Because I need to lie down. (Why I'm lying down.)
- Because I'm having a bad day. (Why I'm taking my knitting with me.)
- Because my head hurts. (Why I'm lying down with my pillow over my face.)
- Because there's no point. (Why I'm getting up.)

Fine Qualities in an Adult

Dear Amanda,

On this day eighteen years ago, I was feeling pretty cocky. You were born, and I sincerely thought I was equipped. I really did. Even though you were my first, I knew my way around babies and wasn't afraid of them, and I was even pretty sure that I had fantastic baby-tending skills. Moreover, this parenting thing seemed to me like it was going to be pretty straightforward. I knew motherhood would have its challenging moments, but overall I thought I was going to be really good at it, and that it would be something I excelled at. I was pretty sure that with all the books I had read and how much research I had done, I would have a great grip on it. I thought that those parents who were losing it all over the place were just not working hard enough at it. I was going to be a relaxed mother.

I think, darling girl, that we can both agree that I have been the exact opposite of relaxed in every way that there is to be not relaxed, and now I really don't know whether to apologize or demand thanks for that. I don't know what went wrong with my plan—my plan for how easy it was all going to be—but when you screamed your way through your first night on this Earth, despite everything the midwife and I could do to comfort you, I started to wonder if I hadn't received a standard-issue baby.

This was confirmed when you screamed your way through virtually every moment of the first four months of your life (thanks for entirely skipping sleep, too; that wasn't at all challenging) and then spent the next several years trying to kill yourself in a new way every thirty-five seconds. At nine months you walked. At ten months you climbed to the top of the fridge and sat up there eating bananas. The moment I walked into the kitchen and found you up there is one that will likely be the last image I see in my mind's eye as I depart this Earth. Sometimes at night I still try to figure out how you got up there.

At eleven months I thought about tying you to the family bed so I could fall asleep without worrying that you would do all of this while my guard was down. At eighteen months you had a full vocabulary with which to add insult to injury; your favorite words were "No," "Not Mum," and "Me do it." Everyone agreed that these choices were very telling. About the same time that you got verbal, you developed a proclivity for biting other children and taking off all of your clothes in public. (Really, no one could help but be impressed with your stripping skills. Fifteen seconds with my back turned in the grocery store and you would be bare-bummed by the apricots, chatting with some stranger. I can't stress how glad I am that you outgrew that.) By age two you had the temper tantrum down to an art form that defeated even your "I've had four children; just try taking me on" grandmother, and you had discovered that your powers had their most devastating effect when you alternated incredible happiness with tornadoes of poor mood so that I was continually off balance and nervous, never knowing what would hit me.

At three years we had to move from our apartment to a house since you had developed an intense determination to leap from the balcony. (You felt that only stupid children were injured in falls. Smart girls landed on the grass and were just fine. Since you were sure you were a smart girl, we moved.) At four you were a good reader and a decent knitter and frequently defeated adults with your keen intellect. By the time you were five, my little prodigy, my life with you was sort of like a game of *Survivor* since there was almost nobody alive, adult or child, who could outwit, outlast, or outplay you.

By six you had discovered the full force of your greatest weapon, your profoundly endearing charm, and by seven we were in the teacher's office at school while she explained that you were the loveliest, most darling child she had ever met but that we were really going to have to help them bring you on board with the system. (What an idea. Why didn't I think of that? I resisted the urge to laugh out loud at her.)

By ten you were off and running in a broad social circle, largely immune to maternal remonstration, and no matter what happened or caught fire or blew up or broke, you kept saying the same thing to me that you always have: "Mum. Relax. I can handle it." I kept a list of emergency numbers in my jeans pocket at all times, just in case you were wrong.

By your teens I spent a lot of my mothering time wondering why you had to reinvent the wheel all the time. (I should have looked up the definition of adolescence and saved myself a little stinking time.) I had already learned everything you were experimenting with. Why wouldn't you just do what I told you? I knew that boys aren't always sincere and that if a girl is gossiping to you about everybody else, you can bet she's gossiping about you to them. I knew that other girl was a liar (and her shirt was totally skanky); I knew what that boy wanted. (Joe knew, too.) I knew that if you procrastinated on an essay you would regret it, and I knew that if you really invested in school your life would be so much easier later on. I knew you would absolutely get caught if you skipped science, and I knew that your supercharm would only save you a few times. Your teen years turned into me following you around trying to tell you all the things I had learned the hard way, desperately trying to save you any kind of pain at all, with you staring at me like I was an idiot who didn't know anything and proceeding to learn everything the hard, painful way anyway. I don't know about you, but I think those years sucked. I think I knit a million pairs of socks trying to keep my mouth shut and take the edge off.

I have spent the last eighteen years being awestruck by the wonder that is you, someone I made in my spare time, and trying desperately to deal best with your epic personality and qualities.

Tenacity. Intelligence. Constructive discontent. Persistence. Sensitivity. A fantastic sense of humor. Independence. Mercy. Fearlessness. Kindness. Equity.

Now, these qualities are terrible qualities in a child. North America wants children (especially little girls) to be polite. Polite, obedient, and pliable, should they be allowed to choose. Kids who fight back and challenge you, say "no," and think for themselves are hard to raise and not thought well of at all. We all talk about how "good" an obedient child is, and it struck me at some point while I was raising you that I really couldn't have a child who did as she was told all the time and then expect you to suddenly turn into an adult who was assertive, independent, and free thinking. I realized you couldn't tell a kid, "Do what I tell you," praise her for obedience, and then turn right around when she becomes a grownup and suddenly say, "Think for yourself" and condemn adults who are still compliant.

In short, I realized that people are adults for a lot longer than they are kids and that it makes more sense to cultivate wonderful adult skills than the traits that make kids easy to take care of. (Mostly I realized this, my child, because despite my best attempts to get some desirable kid traits out of you, you wouldn't do otherwise.)

Over the last eighteen years, eighteen years in which I believe that you and I have tested each other's patience at least once a day, often to the point of tears, I have often gotten through all of them by telling myself, "These are great qualities in an adult. She's going to be an adult longer than she is going to be three (or six, or nine, or thirteen, or fifteen). Do not kill her before she is finished." This strategy has helped me a great deal. (I don't know what strategy you used to keep from killing me.)

Now, after all this, after all those days that I didn't book a plane ticket to Belize because I was holding on to the idea of an adult you, suddenly she's here. You're an adult. A beautiful legal adult who (at least on paper) doesn't need her mother. You can vote. You can move across the country. You can start a business or join the Peace Corps or—mercy, my child, you can do whatever wonderful thing you want, and you can do it all without my permission.

I am scared to death.

Motherhood is the only occupation I can think of where your eventual goal is to put yourself out of business and make it so your customers don't need you anymore, and I have swung back and forth these last few years, hoping one moment that you will leave (I admit, we both probably know what days those were) and wishing the next moment that you will never leave and I will be allowed to try to keep you safe and with me forever.

While I am not sure that I am entirely okay with this growing-up thing, I know now that I have to at least start letting you go a little bit. I need to worry less about you and send you more out there, and I will. (Not all at once, though. The world is freakin' huge.) Please try to be patient with me; it's so hard for me to let go of my job. Try to remember that up until now if something happened to you, it was my fault, and they could put me in prison for it, and in my defense, you are my eldest and the kid I had to practice all of this on.

I hope, dear Amanda, that all of this leaping without looking and enthusiastic going forward has taught you to at least scan the ground a little as you fly, and I'm going to try and trust that you know how to pick yourself up if you land hard after all, all of the things that have made it a challenging, crazy ride to be your mother . . .

These are terrific qualities in an adult. Boldly go, my dear heart. Boldly go.

Poor Planning

As I walk and travel around the city, I knit. Nothing complicated, because I am not so bright as to be able to do anything very complicated while I'm walking, and also because I live in a big, bustling, busy city where nice but rather vacant people who wander around knitting and not looking where they are going are likely to get splattered by a taxi or something. (There was also an incident in which I walked squarely into a pole while cabling, which I prefer not to speak of and would rather you thought of as a "teachable moment.") In light of these urban dangers, and the danger that I am to myself, I keep the walking and transit knitting simple. All I can manage, if I value both my life and my reputation, is a simple stockinette sock, and I do.

When I am walking around the city knitting, I usually keep my yarn in a wee bag that hangs from my beltloop or wrist. It's got a top that gathers up so that when you yank another length of yarn free your yarn can't leap from the bag and land in a puddle or something, and I think these bags are tremendously handy, and in fact I have several of them. This day, as I was leaving the house, I realized that all of my walking-around knitting bags were full of sock knitting that I didn't want to take with me. You know how it goes. That sock needs stitches picked up at the heel, and I can't pick up stitches on the bus because it is too bumpy. The other one can't come because I think it's time to start the decreases for the toes, but I have to try it on before I am sure, and thanks to that day last summer I totally know what people on the bus think of someone who slips off her right shoe and sock and then slips on a toeless sock with a spiky crown of deadly looking needles stuck in it. It's not good for my image, and I understand now that this sort of public behavior is likely one of the reasons why the other parents point at me and whisper at school meetings, but I digress. The point is that none of the other socks would do.

I was also running a little bit late, and if I took even a moment to dump some knitting out of a bag and then put knitting in, then I would probably miss the aforementioned bus, and then I wouldn't get back from downtown in time to get to the school, and frankly, I am tuned in enough with the parenting thing to know that showing up late to get my kid, disheveled, weird, and flushed from running, is probably the other main reason why the other parents point and whisper at school meetings. Determined to get it together and remembering that being late because you prioritized a half-knit sock is not well understood by the rest of humanity, I simply took the sock I wanted to (halfway down the leg; perfect walking and bus knitting) and rammed the yarn into my pocket.

By the time I got to the bus stop near my house, I was remembering why I had bought the wee bags. The yarn wouldn't stay in my pocket. Every so often when I'd pull a length free, the ball would tumble from my pocket, landing behind me. (Not every time, mind you, because that would have taught me a lesson. No, no, this was at random intervals, so my occasional success would keep me trying.) I'd be alerted to the trouble when my knitting was suddenly tugged or even yanked from my hands because the ball was hung up on something behind me, my sock tumbling to the ground or slingshotting through the air, needles glittering threateningly in the sun before clattering to the ground. If the ball didn't get hung up, and the yarn kept pulling neatly from the center of the ball, then it might be rescued by a kindly passer-by who would spot the thing, an everlengthening leash of yards of bright wool, unwinding as I wandered away, happily knitting while trailing three-ply sock yarn through the city. I admit that although my yarn was becoming ever dirtier and vaguely damp, I did love the way that the good Samaritans all said the same thing—"Excuse me? You've dropped your . . ."—and then trailed off, just like the yarn, because they kindly started that sentence before realizing that they really weren't entirely certain what I had dropped. As entertaining as that part was, when three people had handed the yarn back to me in a half block, I decided that maybe walking and knitting just wasn't going to work out today, and I put the needles and sock into my pocket along with the fugitive yarn.

On the bus I braved it for a while, the ball perched on my lap where it couldn't go anywhere (as long as I remembered to put a down with a handful of people inside. I imagined emergency services turning up and eventually freeing them, and then emerging from the utility room with fifty-five yards of my yarn in their hands while exclaiming, "Aha! This is the culprit!" and looking over and seeing me there, the incriminating sock still in my hand. It was going to be like the time I killed the washing machine pump while felting green slippers, then had to stand there guiltily writing a check for $400 while Joe watched the repair guy pull handfuls of green fibers out of it. This was going to be just like that. I stopped hitting the button. Maybe it was better if it just went to the seventh floor and stopped there. Maybe I should tell someone who could keep it there while I tried to explain that they had to find a way to retrieve my yarn before it tied up the whole system. I wondered what the police were going to charge me with. Misconduct? Mischief? Vandalism or damage to property? Oh God . . . the passport office was in this building. Was I on federal government property? The elevator proceeded, yarn passenger alone, all the way to the seventh floor without stopping.

I stood there, looking at the "7" light, and thought for a second. I tried to calm myself down. Surely lots of people have had yarn accidents in and around elevators, right? If yarn were so dangerous as to be able to cripple city buildings and cause expensive damage, they wouldn't just let me carry it around, right? As I stood there, in front of the doors, my umbilical cord of yarn curving from the sock in my hand to the black line dividing the doors, two things happened. First, a few people came up and stood with me, waiting for the elevator, and second, the elevator began to move downward again.

I jumped, startled into action, and decided that I had to at least try to prevent disaster. Now that there were witnesses, I couldn't just stand there. I imagined how my inaction would look at the trial. This round-faced man beside me, up on the stand saying, "And she did nothing, Your Honor, nothing. She knew the yarn was in there and what it could do, and she just stood there," and then he would break off, dissolving into hitching sobs.

This vision of my unpleasant future (a future in which all of my mother's suspicions about the dangers of my wool issues were validated) prodded me into action, and as the incredulous witnesses watched, I tried to reel in the yarn through the crack in the door. I tugged, I pulled, I nervously watched the lights at the top—6, 5, 4—why wouldn't it come? Was it already caught on the mysterious inner workings of the elevator? I smiled nervously at the witnesses, who were watching me with rather astonished faces. One woman's mouth actually dropped open as I worked my hand closer to the door, hoping to ease even an inch of rescue. Down it came—3, 2—and I began to wonder whether I was going to escape. Perhaps when the door opened, the ball of yarn would be sitting there with the yarn simply severed by the door. (Part of me hoped not. I hate weaving in ends.) Or maybe the yards that had pulled free were hanging in a big loop down through the rest of elevator shaft. I could get someone to hold the door open as I wound it all back onto the ball. As long as no harm was done, I might be able to convince these people that I was just quirky and charming, not several mental tools short of a workbox. I glanced around at them. From the looks on their faces I could tell that quirky and charming wasn't quite what I was pulling off at the moment. Never mind. I could recover. The bell chimed, the "L" button lit up, and at long last, the elevator doors made ready to slide open.

I stepped forward, in front of the witnesses, and waited. I prepared myself for whatever I beheld when the door opened. I said a few words of thanks to whatever force may rule elevators, for allowing such a good ending, and I prepared to wind my fifty-five yards of sock yarn back up as quickly as I could so as to not inconvenience anyone any more than I had to. (It was going to be embarrassing enough. I could at least be efficient while I was odd.) The door slid open then, and the tail of yarn that had been pinched between the doors drifted back under its sock and lay there. No one came out. Not a single soul. So the yarn had broken. Well, that was unfortunate but was probably what saved the elevator from doom and me from possible charges. I was rather pleased that I wouldn't have to look any weirder than I already did and could avoid explaining to these nice people that they would be allowed to carry on with their important business just as soon as I was done playing wool games with an elevator.

That's when I noticed there was no wool. The doors had slid open, the tail had fallen out, and there was no yarn on the elevator. I stared, then I jumped in and looked around. Where the hell had it gone? I goggled at the floor. I looked in all the corners. I examined every inch of the floor, inasmuch as it was possible to do so with all those other people getting on. Damn it. The urge to shove a woman blocking my view of the front left corner passed briefly through my mind. I settled for a more normal choice, but I got the impression that "normal" might not have been how I looked as I asked them all to check around their feet for errant yarn. It wasn't there. The elevator began to move again. I couldn't stop looking at the floor. I ran back through the series of events. I dropped a ball of yarn in the elevator. The doors closed, and the elevator went directly to the seventh floor. Presumably, at that point the doors opened, then closed again, and then the elevator came directly back to the lobby. Since no one got off, nobody had gotten on at the seventh floor. So . . . where did it go?

As we rode up in silence, I tried to figure it out. Maybe it had all raveled. No, not far enough, was it? I looked at the sock in my hand and thought for a second. No, not far enough. A pair of socks takes three or four hundred yards, and I was still on the first sock, so at least two hundred yards had been in that ball. Even seven floors of building couldn't use up that much. I wondered whether maybe the end had gotten pulled into a gear (I'm not sure how; when I'm upset my theories tend to be a little loose) and two hundred plus yards of fingering weight merino had been sucked into the work-ings just as I had feared, only now I'd been stupid enough to get on the elevator. I was an idiot. Not only could I end up stuck here for hours, imprisoned by my own wool, but I'd have nothing to do while I waited to be freed except stand there and hold the remaining half sock as evidence. Maybe I could eat it before they got the eleva-tors fixed. I looked at the other people. Damn. Maybe I could eat it secretly. The elevator kept traveling, and I came up with another hypothesis. Perhaps, as the doors closed downstairs, me on one side and the yarn on the other, the yarn had sat in the middle of the floor where I'd last seen it. Then, as the elevator began to move, the yarn had, because the insides were a little bit tangled, you know how they are sometimes, not pulled free smoothly. The line had drawn taut as the elevator moved, and the ball of yarn had been pulled to the seam at the front of the elevator, pressed against the spot where the yarn snaked out. The yarn, under tremendous strain between the two closed doors, had snapped, and when the elevator had gotten to the seventh floor, the second the door that the yarn was pressed up against opened, the yarn had fallen out the opened doors, and down, down, down the gap between them, all the way to a dark and lonely fate at the bottom of the elevator shaft.

Can you get things back from there? I visualized myself trying to explain to the building's mechanic why I needed to go into the bowels of the building, but I knew (after the episode with the subway platform last year) that it probably wouldn't go my way. I tried to imagine some risk to the building that would make them want to retrieve it and give it back to me, but my imagination let me down. As we approached the seventh floor, I reconciled myself to the fate of my yarn. Down the gap to a damp, dark eternity. Mystery solved.

Solved, until a moment later, when I stepped out of the elevator and cast a mournful eye down. I stopped in the doorway. There was no gap, or technically, not one large enough for my ball of yarn to fall down. People went by me, pushing around me on my left and right, and I stood there and stared. No gap. My hypothesis crashed down around me. I straightened, eyes front, and looked at what waited outside the elevator on the seventh floor. A long queue of people spilled out of the passport office and past the doors of the elevator. They stood there, some with headphones on, some looking impatient, some of them gazing off into space. The line wasn't moving quickly at all, so I could guess that these people, or maybe those ones, a little farther up, had been the folks standing here when the elevator door opened three minutes ago with my little ball of yarn sitting in the middle of it. I stepped off, and I surveyed them.

That's when it hit me. One of these people was a knitter. They had been standing here, waiting in the queue when they had heard the elevator bell chime, and out of natural human curiosity, they had looked over to see who was getting off. The door had opened, and there had been my single ball of exquisite handpainted merino sock yarn. They had been stunned. I mean, here they were, standing in line at the passport office, bored out of their tree (I imagined that this would be the one day they had forgotten to bring their own sock to knit with them), and out of the blue, while they were standing there thinking, "Woe is me, if only I had a little bit of sock yarn," and the door opened, and they looked in and saw it. An offering from the elevator gods. They must have been stunned. They surely looked around, decided that if they were quick they might not be caught, ducked out of the queue, snagged the yarn, and resumed their position, clandestine yarn stuffed in their pocket, hardly believing their luck as the elevator doors closed and returned to me.

CHAPTER 4

Left-Leaning Decreases

Stories about Women, Politics, Knitters, and
Looking at Things a Different Way

Ken

I'm not going to describe how my friend Ken knits. Enough people look at him while he does it. He's like a magnet. Everywhere he goes people swarm around him, particularly women. Now, Ken's an attractive guy, but that just doesn't explain the interest women show in him. Young women, old women, knitters and the non-knitting alike, they can't take their eyes off him while he knits. They sidle up to him in restaurants, stare admiringly on buses. They stop walking and come over and talk to him about it, and I know it's not just the knitting that does it, because I knit in public all the time, and all I've ever gotten is the occasional, "Oh, I wish I could knit." Or, "You must be so patient." Now, I'm at least as attractive as Ken, so I know that the attention has to do with the combination of his Y chromosome and yarn. You would think male knitting was Brad Pitt in a thong for how much attention it gets.

Last summer (or maybe the summer before) I sat on a park bench next to Ken, and we both knit. It wasn't an experiment, but it sure got me some information. I happened to be knitting a lace shawl. Very fancy, very intricate—a whole lot of points on the "impressing people in public" scale. Though he is a very competent knitter, this day Ken happened to be knitting something squarish in plain, no bells, no whistles garter stitch. Two women came up out of nowhere and began to fawn over him. They asked him where he had learned to knit and how long he had been knitting. They stood over him like he was a rare bird or a valuable racehorse. They said things like, "That's terrific," "Good for you," and the killer, "You're just amazing." I could have taken off all of my clothes and danced on the bench beside him holding only the shawl in progress over my private bits, and they wouldn't have so much as said "Nice work" while glancing at me.

I know that this is how people behave when we step out of our expected gender roles, but I can't help but be offended. It's insulting, and not to me; I don't mind that they didn't care about my shawl. It's insulting to Ken, and to all men. What does it say about our expectations of their gender that when one of them knits, just as we do, we think they are exceptional or remarkable? As Ken points out, they must think him as bright as bricks if they are so impressed that he's able to manage.

It doesn't stop with knitting; I've noticed that many otherwise bright and astute women have a remarkably low standard for men's behavior, and they don't even know it. There's a woman in our neighborhood who recently gave up full-time work to stay home with her three kids. Daycare wasn't working out for them, and one of the parents needed to take the hit. She did so, graciously and with aplomb. You would think she would be the toast of the neighborhood. You would think the other women would all be talking about what a great mother she was, to see her kids' needs and step up and sacrifice like that. You would think that the other mothers would have made her some sort of award. Instead, as they gathered in the park I heard the sainted mother in question and her friends discussing her husband and how he had gone from playing hockey three nights a week down to two, to give her an evening of "help" now that she had the kids full time. They were all talking about how he was the best father ever.

You could have knocked me over with a feather. Don't get me wrong: I think any parent who makes any sacrifice for his or her child is a good person. I think what he did does make him a really good dad. I just think that we live in a society where because of our low standards, men who give up a night of hockey to care for their own kids are great guys, and women who sacrifice a year or two (or ten) of their careers are simply doing what's expected of them, and their gift of time to their family isn't discussed in the park at all. Frankly, that pisses me off.

There are examples everywhere. We hear people refer to men "helping" with the housework as though women bear the primary responsibly for it, or going home to "babysit" their own children. (Tip: If you never get paid, it's parenting.) Think over how many times in your life you've heard a woman say, "I know that some men are like that, but not my Bob. He helps with the housework a lot.

He's terrific." Then everyone nods and agrees. Bob's a good guy, and he is. There's no doubt in my mind that Bob, and a lot of guys like him, would live up to our expectations if we raised them, especially if we did so collectively. There's only so much we can expect men to do to improve their contributions if we heap praise on them by the boatload every time they do something that we do all the time. We're the ones who are telling them that it's enough. We're the ones telling them that we're so thrilled that they're doing this little bit to break down the rules about the domains of women and men that they are impressed and proud about their contributions already.

Ken is not to be blamed for any of this, of course. He's a lovely man, a fine knitter, and when women fall on him, singing his praises about his ability to do things that women do all the time without getting any accolades at all, he cops to it. He doesn't buy what they're selling, that it's more special when a man does it, that it's wonderful and validating for women to see a man do something traditionally considered feminine, and he sees the injustice of how it all works. He's on my side, and he's the closest thing to a feminist male that you can get, and he's properly insulted by how impressed they are that a man would summon up the brain cells to knit. He knows that he's being held to a different standard, that it's easier for him to be impressive because he happened to be born with his reproductive organs on the outside rather than the inside of his body.

These are old stories, and I don't know what the answer is, but I do know this: Offering men accolades and waxing lyrical when they do the things that women have been accomplishing forever (and usually all at the same time), like parenting, housework, or knitting, even if they are doing more than other men, doesn't do either gender any favors, make the work women do any more valuable, or do anything to help diplomatic relations between the genders. I can tell you that I spent eighteen years at home with my kids, and not once did anyone come up to me and tell me it was fantastic that I had given up not just my pastimes but my job to do it, told me I was a really great person for taking the time to clean the toilet, or told me that it was simply amazing that I was knitting, and although I do think it's grand when a man does those things (mostly because I think it's grand when a woman does those things, too), I increasingly think we need to even up a bit, so here's what I'm thinking.

The next time you see a man knitting, try to treat him like he's not exceeding your expectations or walking on water, even if you are really impressed and sort of have to fake it.

Remember, if you can do it, so can he.

dim nature publicly, but I watch their eyes when I take out my knitting, and I see them do the math. No matter what I was doing before I took out my knitting, even if I had been discussing physics or comparative religion, the minute I pull the stuff out of my bag a look flashes over their visages, and I can tell that part of them just thought it. No matter what they thought of me before, what some of them think now is that if sticks and string are all I need to amuse myself, then I must be very easy to amuse. (I've commented before on how incredibly ironic I find it that they think I'm dim for doing something they themselves cannot do, but that's an argument about perception and their own problems, and we'll gloss over it for today.)

Their concept of me and my attendant acumen is only cemented if the darlings happen to see my stash or if they find out what I paid for it. If you're up for a bit of fun and would like to test this theory, show someone a handpainted skein of yarn and tell them it was twenty-five dollars and that you are going to make a pair of socks out of it. Almost every time, they'll look like you're crazier than a bag of wet weasels and shake their heads sadly (or discreetly) about your lack of intelligence. Some of these dear souls, the ones with poor self-control or less than stellar behavior, some of them will even try to help you understand the error of your ways, pointing out that socks can be had for a dollar a pair with almost no effort at all. (As an aside, I've never understood what they hope to gain from this. They tell me that as if they expect me to exclaim, "Really? Are you serious? Why didn't someone tell me before now? Do you know how much time it takes to make a pair of socks? Oh, woe is me, the hours I have wasted. Thank you, thank you, sir, for telling me this and freeing me from my wretched hours of sock-knitting labor. Please, please, I beg of you. Take me to this mysterious 'Wal-Mart' where I too can obtain these cheap socks!")

When I was a younger knitter, and a knitter with less experience, this used to get to me. There are so many people who don't understand my relationship with knitting that I used to get overwhelmed. As I was growing up, my grandfather used to have a theory. He used to tell me that if one person thinks you're wrong, you can still be right. If two people think you're wrong, you might want to check your facts and the basis for your argument, but if three or more people think you're wrong? You probably are, and you shouldn't let your pride get in the way of seeing that.

Clearly Grampa wasn't a knitter, for if he was then he would have seen that there an exception must be made for activities as widely misunderstood as this one. The culture I live in is chock full of people who think I'm wasting time when I'm knitting. In fact, the culture I live in thinks that watching TV with a bag of chips is a lot more valid—or certainly easier to understand. (Demonstrating that I knit while watching TV and eating a bag of chips hasn't helped me fit in any better.) Nobody wants to stop me from knitting, not many people even care that I'm knitting, but precious few of them think that my knitting is a demonstration of my intelligence or general canny common sense. Perhaps it's a leftover from antiquated beliefs about women and the work they do (especially since men who knit aren't generally regarded as dim—merely effeminate), or perhaps their distaste springs from a general misunderstanding about what's really happening when we knit.

I could explain to them about how knitting uses both hemispheres of the brain at once, I could explain that knitting instructions are a code that we decipher, I could even tell them that knitting has reading and math and can be so complex that it would make them weep, but instead, I think I will tell them about Turkish rugs.

In most early religions, Christianity and Judaism included, women were forbidden to receive religious education. The easiest way to make sure that didn't happen was to make sure they were illiterate or to discourage literacy. (That way, they couldn't get an education even if they were sneaky.) Communication though, is a human need, and human nature will always find a way. The knotted rugs woven by Islamic women in Turkey are a wonderful example.

Each beautiful rug is covered with a series of traditional geometric and repeating motifs, taught from one generation to the next, mother to daughter. As women grow older and their hands become too tired to tie knots and weave the carpets, they become the spinners, helping to provide the yarn needed. As they spin, they teach the younger women and girls the patterns. It seems antiquated, pastoral, and even, much like my knitting, dreadfully simple. All the women take part in the work somehow. Some of them excel, for sure, but the work is so straightforward that few women in the community would be considered too dim to do it. It would be easy to look upon these women and see exactly what some see when I take out my wool and sticks. Women, ordinary women, engaged in an ordinary pastime. The patterns are established. The knots get tied the same way each time. The work appears manual, mundane, and, to our modern eyes, sometimes even a little stupid.

There are faster and easier ways to get carpets. Sure, they are making very special carpets, just as I may be making very special socks, but generally speaking, it is not considered an intelligent way to get carpet. The intelligent way is the commercial way. Big commercial looms churning out acres of sturdy, serviceable carpet that can be scrubbed and installed. The intelligent way doesn't make the best carpet. It makes the most efficient carpet. People might acknowledge that hand knotting, like hand knitting, makes beautiful objects; it does not make efficient objects and is therefore a less intelligent operation.

Here's what they don't know about the simple, mundane women knotting the rugs. They are reading and writing. The human will find a way, and no human is truly illiterate. The motifs and patterns are a language, and anyone who knows that language can read the story the weaver tells. A stylized goddess with her hands on her hips is a motherhood symbol and usually shows that the weaver has given birth to a son. An image of a chest or bag may show the weaver is wishing for marriage and a dowry, lines that represent hairbands show the weaver has married, and a figure may represent a person who is being memorialized and is often woven in a carpet that tells the story of the loss of a child. The sort of border put on may indicate the age of the woman or her children. Stars are life, ravens can be death, a dragon sweeping around might mean the rains were good.

Each carpet bears the story, the wishes, and the hopes that each weaver has, and each motif is passed on in the only written language the women know. Banned from reading and writing the language of their culture, they have written a language of their own. Each carpet is a meaningful, powerful story, each line of knots almost a journal of all that she says and thinks. It is as though these women are writing their lives down, teaching each other their stories, and telling all of us what has happened to them while they were here. These stories persist long after the women are gone, since a well-made carpet can last for many, many, many years. It is a powerful and compelling thing, an incredible and heartening story, and what does it look like?

It looks like a woman playing with some wool. Making knots and creating an item that could be made more efficiently by a machine or obtained more cheaply at a Wal-Mart.

As I have said, I am not a stupid woman. I know how I look when I pull out my knitting. I know what they are thinking when I pull out my wool and what will be some very expensive socks when I am done. I don't care. I'm making a pair of socks that will be on my daughter's feet when she goes to college. I'm making a hat my brother will wear to work. I'm knitting a sweater to warm my husband and a bonnet for a baby who has just arrived and is much loved. I'm telling my story . . . and I don't care if I look stupid or inefficient. I know what I'm doing. It's not my problem if they don't.

A Contradiction of Terms

Imagine this: You and I are sitting together on a park bench, and we are having a lovely time, knitting and chatting, maybe we have coffee and some chocolate. It's lovely. I spread my knitting in progress out on my lap to admire it, you know, the way knitters do, and I smooth my hand over it and give it a little pat just like it's a rare or treasured pet. Then, something catches my eye, and I lean forward to take a better look at the sweater, and suddenly you can see what I see. There's a massive mistake. You inhale sharply; this is going to be bad. This is one of those ugly mistakes that can shorten a knitter's lifespan. You slowly look up at me, prepared to help me through this awful moment, and much to your surprise, I break out in an enormous smile of sheer joy and exclaim:

> *Wow! Look at that! I made a huge mistake way back at the beginning of this sweater. Oh my gosh, it's enormous! No wonder the rest of the sweater looks so odd. My goodness, that mistake is*

as obvious as Cher naked at a convent, isn't it? How did I not see that? Well now. What a fabulous turn of events. I'll just have to rip this whole thing out. Yup, every single stitch except for the cast-on edge is entirely unacceptable! Oh, but I'm so lucky! I'm glad that I got a chance to knit almost the whole thing before I noticed this. If I'd seen that mistake right away, then I wouldn't get the pleasure of knitting this practically twice! Oh happy, happy day.

Having been the knitter who has made a mistake of that magnitude, I think that if I ever heard a knitter say that, I'd either get up and move, consider talking about her in unflattering terms after she left, or, even though I'm a nonviolent person, I think I'd momentarily consider knocking her off the bench in an attempt to smack the stupid right off the poor unfortunate. I can't see any way that anyone sane would talk that way about a knitting mistake and having to reknit something, but if you think about it, that's sort of a contradiction.

I like knitting. I like it a lot. I like it so much that really, if you're going to apply pure objective logic to the thing, I should be absolutely thrilled to have anything happen that creates the opportunity to do more of it. Even better, considering the cost of yarn and the way once it's used up, its knitting value is gone, I should practically dance at the thought of gleaning more pleasure from it by using it twice before it's through. I should feel that way. As an intelligent, thinking person, I really shouldn't think that the idea of "happily reknitting" is as oxymoronic as "smart bomb," "alone together," or the classic "government organization," but I do.

Swatching is another rampaging contradiction for a knitter. I should, if you look at the purpose of the thing, embrace this tender first date between knitter and yarn. Even though it is often inaccurate for the purposes of gauge, swatching still marks the beginning of a knitting project. Since I love knitting and love beginning projects, this first delightful overture between it and me should be a grand harbinger of great things to come. When I sit down to swatch for a new project, I should enjoy every minute of it; after all, it's not as if to prepare for a knitting project, one has to clean the toilet or scrub all the floors in the house. It's knitting. More knitting. Not only am I getting to know the yarn, learning how it feels and behaves, but I am getting an opportunity to experiment with it on a scale that could prevent the reknitting that makes me so unhappy. Despite all of this, I avoid it like the plague. I know that if I skip it, I'll often make things harder for myself; I know that wimping out on the swatch can mean that I don't discover that this piece of knitting stretches to four times its size when it hits water or other disasters that I can't even speak about, they've left me so scarred. Intellectually, I know that not knitting a wee square because I don't want to waste the time could mean that I'll have to reknit a huge square, and I still skip it, and even have the audacity to be angry and frustrated later when there's a problem that could have been entirely prevented had I not taken a long swim in the deep end of the knitterly contradiction pool.

It gets worse. I tell myself that one of the reasons I don't swatch is that swatches lie, and not just a little bit. Swatches have been known to lie at the Olympic level. They can be reliable and useful in driving cars, we'd be walking, on the premise that if you like walking, why wouldn't you do more of it?

It seems to me that in the end I can blame my nonsensical knitter behavior on the fact that my humanity entirely overruns the logic I have about knitting. Knitting, being something a human does, is therefore subject to all the conditions that a human is. I like to think that. I like to think it because the alternative is that I'm not very smart, and that just doesn't seem right. That I'm smart enough to knit but not smart enough to keep myself out of knitting trouble would be another contradiction.

It's all contradictory. Our human nature makes it so that we love knitting, but we don't want to do it unnecessarily, and our human nature makes it so that we embrace innovation and greater goals while throwing up roadblocks to getting to just that place. Human beings are inherently contradictory because our big brains and intellectual selves are in constant conflict with our hearts and emotional selves. It's got to be the answer, because it's that or I've gotten myself into a place with knitting that is really, really sneaky.

All Things Being Equal

Not too long ago, a group of friends and I trundled off on a knitting weekend. We had rented a minivan, packed up our fiber and spinning wheels, tucked in all of our knitting projects, and iced the cake with yarn for trading and sharing. (We may have also added a case of a decent merlot to the haul, but we shall never reveal the exact nature of our good time.) We rented a couple of hotel rooms near a sheep and wool festival and shipped off. We spent the whole weekend going to the festival during the day and spent the evenings knitting, spinning, and visiting with other knitters who had gathered for the same purpose.

Now, these were all sorts of women. One is a doctor, one a nurse, one is a mum at home, and the other owns her own business. Me, I'm a writer and perhaps a knitting philosopher; we're a pretty diverse bunch. One evening, we got to talking about the weekend, and how people responded when we said we were going away for a knitting retreat.

The response was universal. People thought our weekend

immersed in our chosen hobby (or lifestyle, depending on how you feel about our level of involvement) was at best sweet or quirky and at worst stupid. Ridiculously stupid. Although we all tried, there seemed to be no way to convince them that we were doing anything worthwhile. We were thought frivolous, silly women with a funny little plan. Several people confided that they thought a knitting weekend was the strangest thing they had ever heard of. When we told them there were going to be hundreds and hundreds of knitters there, they expressed nothing short of shock.

When we realized that the reactions we had gotten ranged from giggles to incredulity, we started wondering what it was about it that had people so tripped out. We started to draw parallels between what we were doing and what other people did. We imagined what people would think if our husbands had rented a minivan, filled it up with fishing gear and bait, added a case of beer, and headed up to a cottage to spend the weekend sitting in a boat or on a dock, dangling a string in the water, and sitting by a campfire. We sat and spun or knitted, and a contemplative silence fell over us. We'd realized something compelling. Nobody would have thought that was odd at all. Nobody would have thought it silly or strange, nobody would have openly boggled at how they were choosing to spend their time. What was the difference, we asked ourselves and each other. What, if anything, made it different? What made sitting on a dock playing with string more valid than sitting at a knitting retreat playing with, well, string? It seemed to us that they were the same, and the first whiff of an unfair bias wafted through the air.

A few days later, when I was back home, my husband and I were in the car listening to a really popular radio show called *Ideas*. It's a show about all manner of things. Every week they explore a different topic in contemporary thought. Religion, culture, the humanities—that week, the topic was golf. Now, I don't give much of a rat's arse about golf, but I have to tell you that even from the perspective of a nongolfer, who doesn't know or associate with many golfers, this was really interesting and entertaining. The whole show was poems and stories about golf and interviews with people and their relationship with golf. They spoke compellingly about the role golf had in their lives. The relationships they had formed because of golf, the friendships that existed only because they played golf. They talked about traveling from course to course and the power and personal fulfillment that they found in becoming good at golf. One man spoke beautifully about how golf had taught him that there is always more to learn, that just when he thinks he knows it all, there's another course, another club, another shot or stroke, and that in playing golf he had discovered a great deal about himself and the sort of person he was. Another gentleman spoke about how a new set of clubs and a trip to Scotland to golf on a historic course had been almost a spiritual journey for him. A poet spoke of his pursuit of the perfect game. Joe and I listened to people talk about the economy of golf, their pride in golfing well. They said that golf had its own culture and language that was unique to them, and it was at that moment that I turned to Joe and said, "Is it just me?"

"No" replied Joe. "You could substitute 'knitting' for 'golf' all the way through that."

"Then why aren't there radio shows about knitting?" I asked, and I didn't get much of an answer. Maybe he didn't have one, or maybe he just knows when not to get me started. We journeyed in silence for a while then, listening to the show about golf, and when it was over, I asked Joe why he thought golf got so much air time. Not just radio shows, I said; "It's on TV."

"I don't know why, honey, but for starters, I think a lot more people golf than knit. It's just more popular, and you can't fault the media for responding to that."

"Fair enough," I replied, but my heart wasn't in it, and the wheels kept turning.

When I got home, I couldn't let it go. I had gotten a whiff of bias that matched the one that had wafted through the air at the knitting retreat, and I wanted facts. Pure numbers to support or refute what I was thinking. How much more popular than knitting was golf; were the attention and respect justified? Several hours (and two glasses of wine) later, I was sitting stunned at the computer. It had taken me a while to work it out, but I had my numbers, or at least the most reliable numbers I could glean with a high-speed connection. Combining information from the Professional Golfers' Association, the National Golf Federation, and the Royal Canadian Golf Association, it seemed about 30 million North Americans golf to any degree, and only about 6 million golf more than twenty-five times a year. Hunting up the knitting statistics was harder. Much harder. (I ignored that whiff again.) When I'd combined media sources and the Craft Yarn Council, several industry magazine statistics, and a couple of other things and averaged them out, the result was enough to knock your merino off your needles.

Fifty million knitters, or at least people who knew how to knit.

I had to make a conscious effort to keep my mouth from hanging open. I printed the page of data and stomped back to Joe. "More people knit than golf," I said, slapping the paper on the table. "Like, twice as many." I tried to make a facial expression that went with what I was feeling. I failed. I was trying too many emotions at once. Ablaze, bothered, competitive, defensive—I could have come up with one for every letter of the alphabet. I stared at my husband expectantly, like there was something he was supposed to say.

"Are you sure?" he said, taking the paper from the table and beginning to peruse the data.

"Yes, I'm sure," I snapped back. I couldn't believe the whole thing. Even if the numbers weren't reliable (I had found one source that defined a "golfer" as anyone who had ever golfed, and one of the knitting ones called a knitter "anyone who knew how to knit"), they still showed a trend. More knitters than golfers. I thought the whole thing was bizarre. I thought about how many golf magazines and books there were at the bookstore. Way more than knitting, an obscene number more, and the knitting section was always tucked away somewhere untidy and lumped in with crochet and quilting. I was sitting there, steaming, and Joe tried to offer explanations.

Maybe it was that golf was social? I countered with examples of knit culture and pointed out that I and millions of other knitters went knitting with our friends to Stitch and Bitches and Knit Nights, not to mention knitting retreats and conventions and classes. I threw in the sheep and wool festivals for good measure. Perhaps golfers spent more money? He stopped himself on that one. Golfers did have green fees and costs to play, but at least they didn't need to buy a new set of clubs every time they golfed because the last set turned into a sweater when they were done playing. He went on and on, offering a multitude of suggestions. "It's a sport," he said, "you have to learn a set of skills to play it," and I told him to give it up. To just quit it. It was, it seemed to me, just like the fishing weekend compared to the knitting weekend. Golfing and recreational fishing, the kind where you even throw back the fish, didn't even make anything, I pointed out. They weren't even productive. I could acknowledge that both fishing and golf might be fun, that they were the pursuit of human skill and talent, and that I didn't think they were worthless; I just didn't think they were more worthwhile than knitting.

"It's about respect," I told Joe, and I meant it. Nobody tells golfers they're wasting time. Nobody tells fishermen you can buy fish at the store and asks why anyone would bother to do it. At the end of the day, all debates exhausted, the only difference that I could divine seemed to be that golf was done mostly by men and knitting mostly by women, and that made one valid and the other vacuous.

I sighed deeply and looked at my husband, still doing his best to catch up.

"So what you're saying," he said, slowly and patiently, beginning to appear enlightened, "is that you want a radio show?"

"For starters," I said, and I picked up my knitting.

What It Looks Like

I was knitting a pair of pale pink baby booties on the bus when an older gentleman sat down beside me, looked carefully at me and then at what I was knitting, and then smiled warmly and congratulated me on the forthcoming blessed event. I was a little startled, and I think I may have audibly gasped, as for a single heartbeat I was afraid I'd been so busy that I was in advanced state of pregnancy and hadn't noticed yet. When I caught my breath, I thanked him for his kindness and let it go. I suppose I could have corrected him, but I thought he might be embarrassed, it would have taken up happy knitting time, and I'm finally old enough to let other people's mistakes go sometimes. It actually doesn't matter whether a guy on the bus thinks I'm knocked up as long as I know I'm not. As it was, I returned his smile, turned to thinking and knitting, and thought about him.

I feel that I know why he said that, and I know the gentleman is not unkind. He is at worst ignorant and probably merely a victim of a well-worn cliché. It certainly hasn't been very long since a woman of a childbearing age knitting a pair of baby booties was a reasonable social cue. Women, especially well-behaved ones who were going to be very good mothers, all flirted with knitting baby booties. It's how Wilma told Fred she was pregnant on the Flintstones, for crying out loud, and a moment like that has to leave a cultural echo, whether it's a little insulting or not. It's the way stereotypes are born, and knitting has more than its fair share of them.

Now, I am not naive. (Or perhaps I should say I'm not very naive. I have to cop to it a little since I was stunned just a few years ago to discover that the woman down the street who keeps finding things that "fell off a truck" really is actually a criminal, not just someone who has an odd and remarkable talent for finding traffic accidents littered with abandoned merchandise.) As much as stereotypes about knitters (or anybody, really, though I am probably guilty of a few) bug the daylights out of me, I know that they must have come about for a reason. Stereotypes are usually born of a common belief, and common beliefs come about because a majority (or at least a bunch) of the people that you're forming an idea about fit within your concept. The guy thought I was pregnant because a lot of women learn to knit when they're pregnant, and that's true. I know lots of women who think of knitting for the very first time when they are expecting a baby. It's like you're making one thing (the baby) and you think, "Wow. This making stuff sure is satisfying. Maybe I could make a whole bunch of stuff, maybe I could even make stuff for the stuff I'm making," and you're off to the races. Lots of pregnant women start knitting, and all of a sudden a little old guy on a bus is making a logical (and sort of weird) leap. That root of truth gave birth to a broader idea that he's trying to apply to all women knitting.

Now, you and I, we know that none of the stereotypes are all the way accurate, and at worst, they are offensive. Knitters are simply not all women. Knitters are truly not all old ladies, and there are lots of reasons why a woman might take up knitting other than pregnancy (though oddly, I hope the gentleman who congratulated me the other day was responding to a stereotype and the baby booties I was knitting rather than making some sort of statement about my physique). We do not all own cats, and similarly, despite all the booties, warm mittens, and fuzzy stuff we own, despite all of the grandmothers who knit before us, I assure you, we are not all nice. There are nasty knitters, just as there are nasty plumbers or writers or politicians. (Sorry. That last one wasn't exactly a strong example, though I'm sure the opposite is true with them at least some of the time.) There are clever knitters, and funny knitters, and silly knitters (I would especially look out for the ones that are both nasty and clever; they are very slippery), and to tell you the truth, I find the very idea that all knitters are nice rather offensive. It implies somehow that the general consensus is that knitters are sort of a kindly but dim crowd, not really bright enough to be trouble.

Knitters are a truly diverse crowd and (as any yarn company executive would be happy to explain to you after a double shot of rye) hugely unpredictable. There's no demographic. Knitters love acrylic novelty yarns. That's a true statement; the industry sells tons and tons of it every year. Knitters also like natural fibers, with millions of skeins purchased for stashes around the world. Knitters love to knit socks. Knitters find socks too hard. Knitters are old ladies. Knitters are young professionals. Starting to see the trouble? All those statements are entirely true, but they aren't true of all knitters. Other industries have "a type," someone that they know is most likely to buy their product, and they can profile that person like a serial killer and target them specifically. Thus far, all attempts to profile knitters and come up with one character sketch that rings true for most of them have been the leading cause of alcoholism in yarn industry marketing personnel. What frustrates them delights me, since I am an independent observer of the free-range knitter, and this same lack of demographic or profile is a constant joy to me. Not only is it more fun than watching my husband cook (and trust me, that's very fun; he thinks things stop cooking when you aren't looking at them), it's truly surprising. Stereotypes about knitters abound, but the ones our culture holds dearest are the ones most likely to be inaccurate, and as quick as you can say "all knitters are women," or are old, or have cats, or have buckets of free time, or are mothers or grandmothers, then in walks a twenty-two-year-old, straight, dog-owning guy who knits baby booties during football games and when things are slow at NASA.

That said, and all facts established, I have a friend with whom I play a little game called "knitter." We sit in a place that we expect will be visited by both knitters and ordinary people—say a hotel hosting a knitting convention or a restaurant near a busy yarn shop. We take up residence, get a drink, and take out our knitting, and we people watch. We look hard. We try to spot, among the comings and goings of busy humanity, all the knitters. If either of us thinks we see one, we exclaim (or whisper, depending on the background noise), "Knitter!" (We refrain from pointing. It's rude and breaks the rhythm of our stitching.) We are surprised how often we say it in unison.

I can hear you; you're sighing and saying, "Of course you can spot them, you idiots. They are wearing a sweater or a scarf that marks them as surely as the tail of a peacock sets it apart from a chicken," and to be sure, that can be a tip-off. (For the purposes of the game, you do get fewer points for those who are swathed in knitwear. It's too much of a gimme.) But even in the summer, when there is no woolly evidence to give them away, or in the winter in the case of my Canadian home, where everyone is wearing wool, we think instead that we can spot them because they are just . . . different.

Just like the old man who thought he could tell something about me, I think I can tell something about them. That their knitterlyness shows up in the way they walk or move, or in their auras, or the simple look of them. Perhaps I've never even been right, but I like to believe that there is a silent kinship or a wave of connection, some clues that humans can use to figure each other out and find our like, some intangible hint, something that makes us look up and say, "Ah, there's something I understand. There's a knitter."

Then again, maybe my assumptions about these people are just as off as the ideas people have about me, although you'd be surprised how often the person I think is a knitter turns a little and has yarn trailing out of his or her bag.

Knitting Self-Esteem

Some time ago, I had an epiphany. A sudden realization of what seemed to be a great truth, which sounds impressive, but I have them all the time. The last one had to do with the nature of motherhood, which came to me as I scraped dried cottage cheese off the inside of the refrigerator, and I realized that really, I thought that maybe, in some sort of primal challenge thing, our kids were trying to get us to abandon our home so that they could have it for themselves. The one before that had me coming to understand that almost all housework is stupid since it puts you, a free-thinking sentient being, in the service of inanimate objects that don't even care if they are clean, but I digress. This latest one came to me while I was knitting socks, which is so much a higher calling than removing adhered dairy products from an appliance that it just had to yield a better one.

They were very fancy socks, and I was about halfway through the intricate cabling and fancy heel turning when I began to think how much doing exactly this confuses non-knitters. Not knitting in general, but this sort of fancy-pants time-consuming suck of a pair of socks. These socks, which were going to be simply exquisite, were going to be hidden in shoes for almost their entire lifetime. Nobody but me probably would ever get any sort of pleasure out of them. They weren't like mittens, where they were right out in front, and people could see, and they weren't like sweaters, where when you finished you had actual clothes. Spending this much time to make not just good but great hidden footwear was something that non-knitters were always asking about, many of them brainwashed by big-box stores into thinking of socks only as a utility piece of footwear.

Our society likes accomplishment to be right up front. We give awards, write report cards, give performance appraisals, and hold graduation ceremonies and anniversary parties so that people can be told that they are good at things and when they have measured up. The whole system sets you up to be judged by how the people around you feel about what you do, and how they feel about what you do doesn't just have to do with what you're doing. We are all only human, and humanity is almost always biased and judgmental. No matter where we live in the world, the people around you (and you) have internal scorecards, and we all look at each other and add up their points. Clean house? One point. Shaped like a supermodel? Three points. How you're dressed? What you do? More points. As in all judgmental systems, you can lose points, too. For example, I am pretty sure that having a fridge with dried cottage cheese stuck to the inside doesn't work in my favor, and I have long suspected that my hair isn't gaining me much. Also, I may be too short.

find something likable about almost everyone I meet, how I can usually find a way to come to them with compassion and understanding when they fail me, but I have the voice inside me be so critical when turned inward. When I see someone who has made a mistake out in the world, I do not usually (we all have our moments) call them an idiot and point and laugh, but should I make an error in judgment, up she comes, and before I have even a moment to defend myself or prepare, she's called me all number of names, insulted my intellect, and told me (just to ice the cake) that I look terrible in these pants, and my mother has always loved my sister best. That's a lot to withstand, and it's a lot for a person to take, coming from all angles like that. It's hard on my self-esteem and how I like myself, and besides, it's redundant. Being the mother of teenagers means that I already have people to tell me that I don't know what I'm doing.

It occurred to me though, that when I am knitting that sock, my inner self, like society at large, pretty much ignores me, and maybe that's what I'm getting while I'm knitting something like this. It feels like it repairs some of the damage done by this month's cover of *Cosmo* (those can't be real) and my failure to be all that society has laid out. I am a good knitter, if a terrible everything else, and this is a great sock. My knitting self-esteem, I realized, might be a whole lot healthier than my regular self-esteem, and the more I thought about that, the more it made a whole lot of sense. My knitting self-esteem is unfettered by my physical self, the Barbie I had when I was six, or the media's constant messages about the size of my arse, what sort of clothes I wear, and whether or not I wear accessories while I clean my already spotless house and smile while I do it. Knitting doesn't think you need to lose ten pounds, knitting doesn't think you're getting older. Knitting doesn't even give a crap if you get fired or divorced. The only thing that matters in knitting is knitting. You're either doing it or not, you're either right or not, either that is two inches in ribbing or it is not, and I think that's why it's so good for my self-esteem.

When I knit well and make beautiful things or finish things, it reminds me that I'm a winner and a person who gets things done. It's healing and supportive, and I know picking up a piece of knitting and doing something right hundreds of times in a row, or eventually finishing a sweater and looking at how I was competent over and over and over again, I think that's got to start leaking. I think if your self-esteem is a little bit bashed up, then knitting could help you fix that. That maybe if you could change what was possible for yourself in one way, then maybe that would leak into all the other parts of your life. Knitting could be a phone line that rings straight into the kitchen of your inner self and says, "Hello? I just wanted to call and tell you that you're wrong about me. I'm great, and I have the socks to prove it."

Every person I have ever met feels deep down that if the world really knew them, if the world really knew what they were thinking or how they felt or about the mistakes they have made, if someone really found out the deepest, most true things about you, or if your inner self was allowed to make calls out, then all those people wouldn't love you. They couldn't love you really. This feeling is the reason that philosophers and religious leaders, mentors and mothers have been telling their lambs forever that it doesn't matter what you think. It is only what you do that matters. It is enough to do the right thing, or a good thing, no matter what you are thinking, and the message knitting sends to that inner voice in your head is a simple one: "You are competent. You are doing the right thing. You are doing it over and over and over again. You are not making a mistake, and if you do, there is a way out. Good job. Also, great socks. You're lucky to have 'em." And when you hear that, it can resonate and grow through you, and maybe, if you knit enough stitches in a row with that level of clear skill? Maybe the cover of *Cosmo* won't matter to you so much, and you'll tell your husband that it's his damn time to do the dishes because fair is fair and you're worth it. Or not.

Personal growth through the actual growth of knitting. It's proof. It is tiny but real accomplishment, it is order out of chaos, it is usefulness drawn out of string. This is a small power, but one that you have, and as long as you are knitting, you can tell that inner voice to stuff a sock in it.

CHAPTER 5

Make One

Stories of Families, Encouragement,
Ever-Growing Stash, and Small Knitters-to-Be

Megan

My daughter Megan is sixteen years old, and I love watching her knit the way that I loved watching her sleep when she was a newborn. (Megan says I freak her out, but I don't care. As long as I'm keeping her alive and housed, I'll look at her any way I want to.) Megan has grown up into a lot of things that I am not. Tall, for starters. Long limbed for another. Where I am short and compact, Megan is lean, long, and at this age learning to negotiate with all of these inches that turned up so fast. She's all angles as she folds herself up into an armchair with her bright red yarn on her lap and a set of double-pointed needles in her hand.

When Megan knits, it looks like digging. Her left needle lies over her palm, fingers below and thumb on top, the needle held between her thumb and pointer finger as though it were a tiny and effective shovel. Her right hand completes the picture of industry, this hand position almost mirroring the other, her thumbs pointed toward each other, as though she were ready to toss a miniscule salad rather than start a pair of mittens. When she begins to knit her left hand remains largely still, simply holding the needle and stitches as they wait to be knit. Only her left thumb moves, stroking the next stitch of the round forward to the needle tips. Megan's right hand is the big action hand, and stitch in place, thumb on top of the needle, index finger curled beneath, Meg digs the right needle into the first stitch with emphasis, right hand already flicking around the needle to wrap the yarn around and back.

Even at sixteen, the movements of knitting have been repeated so many times that Meg looks comfortable. Her hands move sure and quick and repeat her own personal knitting series so quickly that I know that someday she will knit faster than me; in fact, sometimes her dad suggests that she already does, just to bug me. As I watch her, she looks away from her knitting and watches TV, then laughs with her sister and looks over her shoulder, all while her hands beaver away in a steady, even, almost effortless string. I'm marveling at what this daughter of mine can do, how she was this tiny baby and now she knits socks without thinking, when she drops a stitch, or maybe splits it, and she glances down, stops the automatic nature of her knitting entirely dead, and is frozen as she tries to diagnose the trouble.

It takes a long time, and Meg hunches over her work, poking at things with a long finger, and it's only in this moment of difficulty that I can see any evidence of her lack of experience. A frown crosses her brow as she ever so slowly diagnoses what might have gone wrong. I resist the impulse to say "Oh, give it to me," because

I know I could fix it in a second, and after what seems like forever, Megan finally sees her trouble stitch, and then abruptly she's a wee girl again. Arms akimbo, sticking her tongue out while she retrieves the runaway, awkwardly lifting and moving the needles just like she suddenly finds them unwieldy, long oars, and then, suddenly everything is on track again, she's back to what she knows, and like someone flipped a switch on her labeled "knit," Megan's off at full speed again, fingers flying without a single thought given to the fact that it was her speed that dropped the stitch in the first place.

This small example is the thing about teenagers that makes me crazy, the thing about them that makes everybody crazy. Speed. Either the kid isn't moving fast enough, or she's moving too much, not slowing down to think about what's happening or what the consequences are or even what's going on. There's a certain whiplash in being the parent of a teenager, where you have to find a way not to scream like a berzerker every time the kid slows down to the pace of a snail on sedatives, and ten minutes later you're following them around the house saying, "Hold on a minute. Why are you taking the cordless drill to the park?" or "I know you're excited, but have you considered that this rodeo plan of yours might be a little dangerous?" or "Okay, maybe your teacher is a moron, but is it a good idea to antagonize a moron in charge?" It's a beautiful thing to watch (should the process leave you with enough clear thought for analysis) because this slowing down and speeding up is evidence of what we all want for our kids—the ability to learn—and done right, this teenaged quickstep turns into the more reliable steadiness of adulthood.

It took about twenty years of parenting (eighteen, actually, but I did several kids at once for extra credit) to come to understand that it isn't really the slowing down and speeding up that is driving me crazy with my teenagers. Speed is a symptom of the terrifying truth beneath. I want my kids to even out and quit driving me bonkers with this stuff because on some level I know that the lack of steadiness reflects a lack of solid priorities or a reliable sense of their responsibilities, and that's scary as hell for the grownups watching.

If a kid can't slow down enough to see danger or can't speed up enough to get out of its way, then she isn't safe on her own yet, and yet she is old enough that everything demands that I start letting go and sending this kid, the same kid who just informed me that piercing your belly button is "normal" and "everyone but her" has done it (call me crazy, but I think "everyone" might be an overstatement), out into the big world alone, where she can make even bigger mistakes and get anything she wants pierced. My husband has a little sign in his office that says, "Quick, hire a teenager while they still know everything," and that's the bigger part of the trouble. You have this kid who's speeding up and slowing down at seemingly random moments, working hard to solidify priorities and morals that are still developing, and the kid has no idea. Not only does the kid think that she has all the answers, but she thinks that you, as an adult and a parent, are a great big wanking idiot who is to be ignored at all costs.

Any normal parent placed in this position is going to want to do one thing, but unfortunately, building a cage in the basement to house your teen until she grows a brain is illegal. I've settled on mistake, and there are moments when the sloth lurking inside every teen takes over and she problem solves at the rate of a two-year-old who missed naptime, but mostly my Meg knits at an even, constant speed that belies her stop-and-start nature and the fickle aspects of her adolescent pacing. Everything that teenagers are—unruly, unfinished, too slow or too fast, too stupid or too smart, the way they know everything and have to reinvent the wheel all the time—all of that is absent in Meg when she knits. When Meg is knitting she is neither rushing nor dawdling, hurried nor absent. She is pure forward, effective movement, her body and hands doing nothing that is unnecessary. All of her is productive, and confident, and steady, and sure. All of her is beautiful. All of her is adult.

Megan's knitting is a hint, a window on her future, a crazy sneak preview of the sort of woman that she will be, should we survive each other, all crystallized in this one perfect moment when I watch my Megan knit an extraordinary pair of warm, red, $17 mittens.

Quick, a Baby Sweater

If you live in Canada, it's incredible what happens in the spring. You would expect part of it. The part where the snow melts and the birds come home and tulips and pussywillows appear from out of nowhere, that's to be expected and doesn't really come as a surprise to us Northern types. Despite the death of hope when it's still freezing in March, we do believe that spring will eventually come. Spring, and with it the liberation of just tossing on a sweater if you need to go outside, the quiet relief that it's finally warmed up enough that if you lose your keys you won't be killed by exposure while you're looking for them, all of that you expect. What I never expect is the sudden plethora of surprises in your neighborhood and among your neighbors.

All winter long people are in their homes, sequestered from the cold. We don't stand on the sidewalk and talk to our neighbors, we don't chat on the porch in the evening. If we do happen to catch a glimpse of each other, we're all so bundled up that unless you can see what house someone goes into, you might not even be able to tell who they are. (I spent one whole winter thinking that a neighbor was having an affair with a strange man until I bumped into him while salting the sidewalk. It was her husband. He just had a new coat.) We are wearing hats, scarves, sweaters, coats, extra socks, gloves, and mittens, layer after layer of clothing. It renders people pretty indistinguishable from each other, unless you happen to recognize their knitwear. (One of my daughters got busted for skipping school in mid-January when she was identified at a distance—and with a scarf obscuring her face—because she was wearing a handknit hat that the rat who finked on her recognized as my work.)

There is a chance you will get a look at a neighbor around the holidays, but frankly we're still wearing a lot of layers against the bitter Canadian cold, and there are many months of winter after December. Suddenly, spring comes, the world peels a layer off, and all of us are stunned to discover winter secrets. The woman who moved in next door in February is actually a guy named Rick, or maybe your neighbor Bob takes off his coat, and holy cow, he's lost twenty pounds over the winter. (Or gained them, which is a little more common with the holidays and hibernation in there.) Children are taller, teen boys have grown whiskers, teen girls have sprouted figures, everyone's hair is longer, and in my personal favorite, you discover the woman you've been talking to at the elementary school every single morning for five months when you drop off your kid has had a big secret under her parka. She's eight months pregnant, and whammo, you need a baby sweater, or booties, or something, and you need it fast. The winter has robbed you of the traditional stuff was fun, I thought, and I even let the idea of doing some of the Christmas knitting ahead of time this year cross my mind, just so I could have more of this good feeling. We stood and chatted, talked about her due date (two weeks, but what did I care?), and laughed about how funny it is not to be able to know these things in the winter. "You would think," she said "that no coat could hide these two!" She patted the broad expanse of her belly.

"Two?" I said, beginning to feel slightly less smug and perhaps a little nauseous.

"Oh yes," she said. "It's twins!"

How to Make a Hat if You Are Twelve (and Not Very Careful about Stuff)

Step 1. Do a gauge swatch, then measure your head and do the math. Then have a fight with your mother, who has knit like, 10 million hats and indeed has written books about knitting. Make the argument about who would know better how many stitches to cast on. Insist that you would be the expert. Glare at your mother for daring to have an opinion. Never, ever admit that your mother may be halfway intelligent; eventually cast on the number she suggests but do so in secret. Do not speak civilly to your mother for some time.

Step 2. Begin knitting circularly but pause to have a fight with your mother, this time insisting that you are knitting garter stitch, because you are knitting every row (and your mother admits that she told you that garter stitch means knitting every row). Refuse to entertain the suggestion that circular knitting may be different from flat knitting, and again insinuate that your mother knows nothing about knitting. Maintain the fight until your mother looks sort of twitchy.

Step 3. Tell your mother (who is pretty freakin' annoyed at this point, partly because of the repeated inane hat fights but also because she has not been alone, not even to go to the bathroom, in days and days) that the hat seems "sort of twisty."

Step 4. Even though you have not listened to one word your mother has said to you in days, and even though you have never, ever just accepted something that your mother has said without challenging it and asking for an explanation, even though there is not one molecule in your body that believes that your mother could be right about anything, when your mother tells you that stuff on circulars is like that sometimes until you get an inch, inexplicably choose this time to believe her, question nothing, and walk away.

Step 5. Return to your mother the next day. Come to her when she is tired, has a limp from spinning, has a work deadline, and has just poured her first glass of wine. Be sure that this time is long after your expected bedtime. Come to her when she is weak and her resistance is low. Come hostile, and come loud. Show her the hat, which is now very, very twisty.

When your mother bursts out laughing, trying to say something about "Join, being careful not to twist," darken your expression and scream, "This is all your fault" and make all sorts of statements that begin with, "You said . . ."

Step 6. When your mother tells you that there is no way out of this, that it has to be frogged, threaten a meltdown that makes Hiroshima look like a minor problem.

Step 7. Insist that your mother fix it or you will never knit again.

Step 8. Watch your innovative and clever mother thread the hat onto waste yarn, sew up and down a row of stitches, and cut between the lines. (Refuse to learn the concept of steek if at all possible, even though it is right in your face.) Important note: Even if you think it is a good idea, resist the urge to say so. Try instead to insist that it will never work, even while it is working.

Step 9. Refuse to participate as your mother threads the hat back onto needles. Briefly smile, looking for all the world like a happy and content child, but hold the bitterness you feel for your mother deep in your heart.

Step 10. Despite the fact that your mother has rescued you from your knitting disaster, immediately begin another fight with her, this time about how you can no longer knit the hat circularly. Mock her during her counterargument about how you were at the decreases and were going to have to switch to needles anyway and maintain that as usual, your mother has sucked the joy out of your life. Stomp away angry. Continue being a normal twelve-year-old, being sure to leave your mother emotionally tattered, exhausted, and confused.

Dear Nana

Mum told me to go send you an e-mail thanking you for my birthday sweaters that came in the mail after I did my spelling but before I went for a bath so I am. Thank you very much for the sweaters. I like the blue one with the dog on it and the green one is a good color, but I think it might be itchy but Dad says he has been wearing your itchy sweaters his whole life and just to put a turtleneck under it so it doesn't touch me. That's what I will do I think.

I think this is a big sweater year for me because you sent me two and Randy gave me one, except for there was a train in the box too and he said that his mom gets sweaters at the store not knits them and I asked him why but he didn't know. Also, Mum is knitting me a sweater, except hers is taking a long time and yesterday when she was trying to make the sleeve part she held it up against my arm and it was too short. Then she said a bad word and I told her that she had to put a quarter in the swear jar and she said that maybe she would just put a five in there because I grow faster than she can knit and now she doesn't have enough wool. She laughed, but I don't think she really thought it was all that funny. Also, I grew out of my boots.

Dad said to her that it was nice that you had sent two sweaters to me for the winter because at the rate Mum goes maybe I wouldn't have her sweater until the summer, and then Mum said that it must be nice that you have all that free time to knit and keep your house cleaner than our house and Dad said don't start with that and Mum said, "Oh, I'm not starting," and then she got a glass of wine and said she would be knitting in the bedroom and Dad said maybe it was a good time for Mum to have some time to knit so he will read me a story. Now he's cleaning the kitchen because that is always what he does after him and Mum talk about you.

I'm going to have my bath now. I got mud on my hair climbing trees. Mum said she didn't know there was mud in trees and neither did I.

See you at Christmastime. I will wear your sweaters until my other one is finished because I think Mum will like me to wear hers too. It is costing her a lot of money in the swear jar.

Love, your grandson,
Michael

P.S.: I think I almost have enough sweaters if you wanted to do something else for the next present.

That system imploded last year when Joe began working from home and the girls hit a year where I have one in middle school, one in high school, and one in college, and I haven't been alone for months. It's like they've suddenly arranged to tag team me, making sure that I don't have a solitary moment. I've searched the house for the secret schedule I know is here, because it's just not possible for them to have achieved such total perfection and coverage. The other day I got up, and so did Meg and Samantha. They left for school, and I sat at my desk, only to hear Joe up and about moments later. It took him a couple of hours to make his calls and get himself sorted, and he walked out the door at 10:30, which in a remarkable coincidence was the time that Amanda's alarm was set for. He went out; she got up and began her daily ablutions, then settled in to prepare her breakfast and study for an exam, taking a twenty-minute break to go buy some school supplies she needed, which she must have prearranged with Joe, since that's when he came back to the house for lunch. Joe and Amanda exchanged sentry posts at 12:30, when Joe went back out to a gig and Amanda returned to use the phone and Internet and generally be in my way until 3:20, when she left for a late afternoon class. In what can only be described as an organized assault, 3:20 happens to be the time Meg gets home from school. Meg blew in with a pack of teenagers who ate everything in the kitchen (although I don't know why the sight of the prostrate writer sobbing in the next room doesn't put them off their food) and then announced they were going to the pool for swim practice and blasted out the door at 4:00, just in time to say hi to Samantha. Sam told me about her day, then sat down to practice electric guitar until the whole family returned for a nice quiet evening around 6:00. Try and tell me that sort of coverage is a coincidence. It just can't be. I have no idea why they would come up with a strategy that ruins the intellect and will to live of the person providing them with food and money, but I suppose it all may be part of a larger plan that I just haven't come to understand yet.

While this system makes me absolutely wild at the best of times, the collusion of the whole family to keep me from writing makes me simply frantic as I approach a writing deadline. This time, I had a book (this book) due in just over a month and was falling behind on the work, mostly because of a crazy idea I had that I would be able to work a few hours a day. When I realized that the kids were about to go on winter break and would be home (in some combination or permutation twenty-four hours a day for ten days), I may have just about lost it. At that point, further time was taken from the writing schedule and lost to abject hysteria and closing doors more firmly (I hate to call it slamming) than was strictly necessary.

At this point, Joe had a masterstroke. He realized that if the book was going to get finished and I was going to be more than a mere husk of my former self, I needed some real time to work, and work in a way that didn't threaten the stability of everyone within a ten-mile radius. He decided I needed to be alone. (I maintain to this day that Joe's best ideas spring from self-defense, this particular one from the very subtle hints I was giving him about my needs. Hints like me taking my laptop into the closet and dimming my screen so as not to be discovered, and the really understated way I kept screaming, "If I cannot get some time alone, this book will never be finished!"). He realized that he had a client who was sort of broke but wanted Joe to engineer and produce a record for him but was a little short on the traditional wherewithal. Joe happened to know that the guy's family has a place in the woods, far from everywhere, a place where a writer could really get lonely and bored, and he worked out a trade. The guy got the start of his record made, and I got six days in the middle of nowhere in the dead of the Canadian winter.

When I say "nowhere" I don't mean it as an offense to the place, and I don't mean it was somewhere unimportant. It was a place in the woods where there was only a woodstove, electricity, and phone, and nothing for miles around. It sat in the center of about ninety acres, and if I wanted to see another person, I would need to hike a half mile to the road, then over four miles to the store, which was one of those crazy little stores that was the town liquor store, beer store, coffee shop, grocery store, post office, and gas station all in one small building. (The population of the entire township, if you add together all forty-eight towns, is just over nine thousand people. I don't know how many of them are knitters.) Here I would be a solitary writer, to almost a scary degree.

I was so thrilled to be going that I packed with a lot of glee. I didn't bring a lot of clothes because I really intended to just sloth around in cozy old sweaters and a pair of yoga pants until the writing was done, and I relished the idea of being so free that I didn't even have to expend the energy to put on decent clothing. (Every member of my family would tell you that this differs in no way at all from my ordinary days, when I sloth around writing in some of the world's most tragic clothing, but the point of the cabin was that it would be appropriate.) In place of clothes, I packed, as I always do, a lot of yarn. A lot of yarn. I was going into the woods for six days, maybe eight, if the weather kept me there, and I brought enough yarn for four pairs of socks and an entire sweater, all of which, I am ashamed to tell you now, I thought I would complete while I was there. (Also, when you are a day's hike through the forbidding snow to the closest yarn store, you want to make sure you've got your back covered.) No kids, no husband, no nothing. I would just be knitting and writing, writing and knitting. That could take a lot of yarn.

Joe's client drove me up to the place, lit a fire in the woodstove, showed me around a bit, and split. The moment he left, I was giddy. Giddy and truthfully, a little bit scared. Not only was I more alone and isolated than I have ever been in my life, I had also, as my mother said, left all my excuses at home. If I couldn't write in that environment, there would be nobody to blame but myself. She was right, and I found that one of the most frightening things I had ever heard, but sort of inspiring. After all, it was in my best interest to write well and prolifically while I was up there so that on my return I could continue to blame Joe and the children for all my problems and avoid any personal responsibility.

It didn't take long for it to work. Deprived of a TV, a radio, company, and other places to go, I was soon bored and lonely enough that I was writing. I was writing a lot. I was writing to entertain myself, to pass the time, to keep a record of what it was like to be in that place. I wrote all the time. After a few days, though, I was surprised to notice a shocking side effect. I wasn't knitting.

Let me rephrase that. I wasn't knitting much. (I don't know if it's strictly possible for me to go cold turkey.) I was writing and going for hikes in the woods and meandering in the snow. I was communing with deer and keeping an eye out for bobcat. When I wasn't out traipsing around listening to trees and negotiating the huge amounts of snow, I was back in the house, tending the fire, cooking for myself, and writing, writing, writing.

The more I wrote, the less I knit, and it wasn't just a matter of time or feasibility, although there is an obvious problem in not being able to physically knit and type at the same time. I wasn't called to it. I didn't need it (much). Generally, I carve several hours out of my day to knit. I knit while waiting, talking, watching TV. I knit on the bus, while I'm on the phone—all the time. At the house in the woods I just didn't have a lot of those things. There was no TV. I wasn't waiting for a bus. There was no downtime, and furthermore, nobody was around to piss me off or annoy me. I've always known that I use knitting to take the edge off of difficult people or situations, and at the cabin I didn't need the edge taken off of anything. As though to confirm this, I noticed that the only time I really wanted to knit was in the evening, when the night closed in all around that place in the woods, the dark pressed up close to the windows, and things got a little bit creepy.

I have long struggled with the question of whether knitting is truly creative. Creativity is usually defined as the generation of ideas, whether it's for art or science or what have you. When you are creative, you're relying on your own brain to come up with answers, solutions, and concepts. In this way, creativity can be found in parenting, plumbing, painting, baking, or even some of knitting. I say "some of knitting" because not all knitting is creative, using the traditional definition. The generation of the idea is creative, and so may be choosing your colors and coming up with your plan. We creatively problem solve in knitting all the time, but the act itself, actual knitting, that's not tremendously creative. That's execution. Once you have the figuring done, or when you're following someone else's pattern, the knitting part of making something just can't be defined as creative, can it? When I think of the process of a plain sock, knit a number of times until it's rote, I'm thinking of the tens of thousands of stitches it takes to finish that sock. When you're just executing knit or purl stitches, repeating them thousands of times, can the physical process of knitting that 96,890th stitch really be considered creative?

The interesting thing I seemed to be learning at the cabin is that the answer seemed like it might be "yes." It was as if I had a set amount that I needed to create each day, and that need could be met by either knitting or writing. If it was turning out that the need to knit was filled by writing, a complex creative process, then mustn't that mean that knitting is, too? I was stunned to discover that they could stand in for each other. (I shouldn't have been. I have known for a long time that knitting is my favorite procrastination to fill hours I should be writing.) If both could satisfy the same urge, then they must be the same sort of process, but (I hate it when I argue with myself) they aren't the same. Writing is pulling a new and thoughtful idea from nowhere, and unless you're also designing, knitting is mostly execution. What my common sense was telling me and what my experience was showing me really weren't matching up. That happens to me a lot, and it usually means I'm wrong about something. (I'm wrong a lot, too.)

On a long tramp through the woods, I got to thinking about it. If I was getting a result that didn't make sense, then maybe I was starting with the wrong base premise. I stood in a snowbank as realization swept over me like a tidal wave. I was thinking too narrowly. Surely knitting and writing both met other needs, needs beyond my need to be creative. They were multitaskers, doing more than one thing, fulfilling more than one purpose. The same way that a glass of milk is both good food and good drink, knitting and writing must be serving another function. Standing there, with the snow melting through my boots, thinking about going back in the house and making either socks or a book, I got it.

It was so simple that I was almost ashamed that it had taken all day to put it together. Knitting wasn't always about creativity, and neither was writing; it was about creation, bringing something into being. Making a thing where there wasn't something before. When I was writing, I was coming up with an idea, and then using my skills to make it a reality. Same thing with knitting. I was imagining a sweater, or socks or whatever, and then using my skills to translate that image in my mind into a real thing you could touch and see. I had been right (and rather wrong) the whole time. They were the same, they fed the same human need, they enriched the soul the same way. They were not an act of creativity, they were a pure act of creation.

Who knew. To your spiritual self, writing a novel may be exactly the same as knitting a sweater.

A Knitting Class

The lady on the phone seems to have no idea that she has said something completely insane, so I wonder whether I heard her right. "Can you repeat that?" I ask, trying to keep the fear out of my voice and to ignore the sound of blood rushing rapidly out of my head, which seems to be interfering with my hearing.

"I'd like you to teach a knitting class at my toy store," she repeats. "There will be about eight kids between five and nine years old. Can you do it?"

Now, that's what I thought she said, and she doesn't seem to think that it's fundamentally crazy, so for reasons that I still can't explain and are completely against my better judgment, I agree.

The minute I hang up the phone I regret the decision, which was not really a decision but a crappy defense against a precision surgical strike. I am one of those people who will agree to just about anything if you ask me directly, and I have a feeling that this woman knew it. Not only do I know that I meant to say "no" when I actually said "yes," I also know that this toy shop owner has burned through three decent upstanding knitting teachers before me, including a friend of mine who is such a good teacher that it's likely that she could teach your cat to not just use the toilet, but to use toilet paper, wash her paws, and flush afterward. Knowing this, I should have said "no."

I imagined what it would be like to teach knitting to that many kids. In truth, I wondered a whole bunch of things, and since I had never taught even one kid to knit, I wondered whether my imaginings of total chaos were going to be that far off the mark. I phoned a friend and told her what I had agreed to do, and hung up when she still hadn't stopped giggling helplessly through an entire cup of coffee. This cemented my belief that if I escaped from this experience (eight kids? in one room?) without being tied to a chair with my own yarn and needles, I was going to think I had done pretty well.

I think that this toy-store owner, the one who had roped me into this, had gathered some empirical evidence and decided I was a good mark because all my children knit. (I also think she was running out of knitting teachers who were not wise to her scheme, but I digress.) On the surface, that would make it seem as if I was a good person to teach kids to knit—after all, I managed to produce three knitters out of three ordinary children—but the truth is, I didn't teach my kids to knit. Nobody did; they were the product of a complicated, multiyear, knitting, learning experiment.

In the 1980s the whole language approach to learning to read became popular. In essence, proponents of whole language believed (and I am oversimplifying here) that you didn't need to teach a kid to read at all. They believed that reading and writing would occur naturally in children when they were ready, simply by involving them adequately with language. Reading to them, showing them writing, generating learning opportunities from a rich literate world around them was supposed to grow readers and writers out of kids, and for the most part those proponents were right. Exposed to enough language sources, kids did learn to read and write, although opting out of traditional language rules meant that they were weaker in some areas than in others. Whole language kids tend to be crappy spellers, for instance.

If immersing your kids in language could make them readers, I wondered, what would happen if you immersed your kids in knitting? Would they learn? Would they accept it as "something Mum did," or would they think it was something everyone did and therefore take it up themselves? Would they come to accept that knitting was just what people did while they watched TV and feel empty and sort of itchy if they had come of knitting age and their hands weren't busy? I devised a plan. Step one was to have some kids. That was pretty easy. I was able to make them from materials found around the home, although it did take some time. Once I had procured the children, I began my endeavor, immersing them in knitting during their formative years.

I knit without cease during this crucial time. I knit them blankets while I was pregnant. I knit while I was in labor. (Useful tip: It is time to call the midwife if you can no longer knit two together without arsing it up.) I knit while they lay nursing on my lap, I knit while they were in the bath. I knit in the park, I knit at playgroups. I knit while they sat on my lap and told me stories, and I knit through temper tantrums (theirs and mine). I even sacrificed fun and empowering experiences such as vacuuming and scrubbing the toilet to free up more knitting time. Inasmuch as it was possible, I put down the knitting only to administer first aid and hugs and to read to them. (It was insurance for the whole language thing. I didn't want to raise a whack of illiterate knitters, even if they were very good knitters. If nothing else, they would need communication skills to search for patterns and yarn on the Internet.)

I swathed my children in knitwear. (Luckily, we are Canadian. This program would have been a little harder to pull off, bordering on cruel, if we had lived in Mexico City.) I made them hats and mittens; they wore wool soakers over their cloth diapers. I wrapped them in woolen blankets and knit cotton sun hats. (That was my concession to our brief summer.) In the immortal words of Elizabeth Zimmermann, I immunized them against the itchiness of wool by starting with the softest, buttery baby yarns and working up to coarser Aran wool. I strategically placed significant knitting books and patterns around the house, and I made sure they understood the importance of handmade things—not just knitted but crafted in any way. To help them understand the value of human time and effort, I implemented "Find Your Own Food Fridays" as soon as they were old enough to make a cheese sandwich. (Feel free to take any of these ideas for your very own. We parents have to stick together.) I put small but beautiful baskets of yarn and needles in their rooms in case they were inspired. I let them use yarn for anything they wanted. Sure, the other mums thought I was odd. Sure, they thought I was a slacker with a messy house who took her kids to the park for hours just so she could sit and knit, but they didn't understand the grand plan. They didn't know about the experiment. (They were still finding value in housework. I had evolved.)

I knit. I made more babies (three in total) at respectable intervals . . . and I waited, and I waited.

As with all gradual processes, there was not a eureka moment. I do not recall the moment that any of them learned to knit; in fact, there is a very good chance I wasn't present at the time. One morning, when my eldest daughter was about five, she asked me for some wool. I supplied it (you cannot withhold the building blocks of a woolly education) and asked what she was going to do with it. "Knit another dolly blanket," she replied. "I used up my bedroom wool." And off she went. I staggered. I was agog. Another dolly blanket? Another?

I followed the miss into her room and sure enough, there was a piece of knitting. It was not a good piece of knitting, I can't say that. I know that this would be just the most perfect story ever if the blanket she had knit was even and beautiful, but it wasn't. It was lumpy. It had stitches that came and went. It appeared that she had cast on by simply winding her yarn around the needle (turns out that works, by the way) and she had cast off by simply pulling the yarn through the stitches at the top in a straight line. None of this, of course, was the point at all. She had knit. This first charming clever girl of mine, only five years old and with no help from anyone, she had knit.

It was a triumphant moment for me. Truly great. I had created a knitter, and an intuitive and clever one at that. It was as though, in that moment, I had reached some sort of a zenith, as a mother and as a knitter, and I was genuinely happy. (It took a while before it hit me that making a bunch of people who wanted my yarn was not going to be a good move for me, but I digress again.)

Years went by, and my other two children spontaneously learned to knit as well. All three of my children suddenly became knitters around the same time that they learned to read. While this sounds remarkable, that children could learn something without being taught, remember that this is how children learn almost everything. Talking, singing, walking, and running, children learn these things, mostly, even if their parents are raving incompetents. (I don't know about other mothers, but I find that very reassuring.)

My children did, after careful, direct exposure, learn to knit. They learned it the way that most of us have a pretty good idea of how to drive before we sit down at the wheel. They learned it the way that we know what a waltz looks like, even if ours is sloppy. They learned it because they had lived it, and they just knew how. It was the way the children of fishermen know (mostly) how to fish. It was the way that farmers' children know how to plant. It was just in them, somehow, through the process of osmosis. They were smart, resourceful children, and after all, knitting is not exactly rocket science. There are only two stitches, knit and purl, only two movements to learn to make. All of my kids had names they could write by then, and all of them were longer than two letters. If they had the coordination to write their names, the intelligence to read, and the patience to bug me to give them a cookie for twenty minutes straight, why was I surprised that they could knit?

I thought then about what my kids had learned and how easily they had learned it. I thought about the natural gifts of human beings. Dexterity, cleverness, being good with code and symbols. I thought about how hard it is for a child to learn even to write her name, and I began to think that maybe I had been wrong about this knitting class. That maybe all I needed was to go down there and facilitate knitting, not ever really teach them to knit, you know? Just lead them to it and watch the magic happen. Maybe I needed a little faith in these children, in knitting and in myself. I gathered up some yarn and needles, I straightened myself out, threw back my hair, and dammit, I went down to the toy store. What kind of a woman is afraid to teach some little kids to knit?

A smart one. That's what sort, let me tell you.

Three hours later I was home with a cold compress on my head, shattered nerves, lessons learned, and an agreement between the toy-store owner and me that perhaps I was not cut out for this work at all. Nothing about my experiment with my kids had prepared me for the experience of trying to teach knitting to a bunch of kids who have not been raised since birth to be ready for it. Here is what I learned in my brief journey as a children's knitting teacher.

- Knitting is easy.
- Knitting is hard. I know it seems contrary to have learned those two things at the same time, but it's all about who is

doing what when. I can promise you that the kid who finds it easy will inevitably be seated beside the kid who finds it hard, just to guarantee a little bonus conflict. There's only so much a seven-year-old who is trying to knit can take from the cocky eight-year-old next to him, purling away.

- I used the knitting poem "Up through the front door, Dance around the back, Down through the window, and Off jumps Jack," and it made all the difference in the world to help the kids remember the steps in a knit stitch.

- Although that poem and others like them really do help kids remember how to make a stitch, they lead to hard-hitting, non-knitting questions like "Who is Jack?," "Where does he live?," "Is it the same Jack as the beanstalk?," and, in the case of one charming little girl who leaned forward when I got to the end of the poem, "What happened to Jack after that?"

- Kids get yarn for free. I don't know why this is, but it seems to be something I can't duplicate in my own life. It may be because they are cute, or maybe because they are tricky (or maybe because they use their cuteness to trick you), but if you are six years old someone will give you all the yarn you want. (It may also be because fellow knitters see the opportunity to bring a child over to the dark side, and if all it takes is a couple of balls of yarn, then that's a small price to pay for the creation of a full-blown, life-long knitter.)

- A seven-year-old boy in a class with his nine-year-old sister will find it impossible to resist the urge to poke her with a knitting needle. She will likely retaliate by snatching his remaining needle out of his knitting and dropping all his stitches. It is probable that he (having been infuriated and provoked by knitting insult) will respond by throwing the ball of yarn attached to the knitting of the child next to him at his sister, thus invoking the wrath of his wee neighbor harpy, and in mere moments the whole knitting lesson will degenerate into some kind of a scene that makes *The Lord of the Flies* look like a tea party for princesses. Separate siblings. Stay on your toes. Put down revolts swiftly and surely. Don't ask me how I know. I'm still not over it.

- Consider plastic rather than metal needles. Consider that metal needles can conduct electricity. You know, in a worst-case scenario.
- If a child knits it himself, no matter how terrible the yarn is, he will never, ever think it is scratchy.
- If your child knits it for you, it will be extra warm.
- I still believe every child is capable of knitting. However, I may be capable only of teaching them one at a time, and only in my natural habitat. Please don't make me go back there.

CHAPTER 6

Continue to Work Even

Stories of Perseverance, Boredom,
and Overcoming

Rachel

Even though Rachel is one of my knitting friends, and mostly when I see her it is either Knit Night or a knitting event, lately I don't see her knit a lot. In fact, when I closed my eyes to imagine her knitting so I could write about it, what I came up with was a series of other images. Rachel laughing, Rachel opening wine, Rachel handing someone a gift that she'd found for them and picked up just as a little treat, or Rachel snuggling a baby so that the mum can have a little knitting time. I know Rachel knits. I've definitely seen her do it, and she has lots of knitted stuff that proves that she gets it done. She's even a good and competent knitter with a great many skills. When I mention this to Rachel, that I don't see her knit a lot at Knit Night, she laughs and calls herself an impostor.

Rachel knits just enough, she claims, to get into the club. She's all about the people, because knitting has given Rachel more than it's given most of us, and that's saying something, since I like to call knitting the gift that keeps on giving.

Rachel has always been bright, vivacious, pretty, and a general go-getting problem solver. She has a startling ability to give people exactly what they need, and you would be stunned at her level of organization. She'd be the last person to tell you how valuable she is as a friend, an employee, or a mother but the first to tell you she had a terrible struggle with depression.

On the outside, it looked as if Rachel had nothing to be depressed about. She was married, with a really terrific son and a great job. She had a lovely little house and a car, her bills were paid, she was skilled at everything she took on, and she was naturally thin at thirty-five. That's a lot to be grateful for, and Rachel was grateful, but all was not as it seemed. All this success was also a trap. She hated her job but couldn't leave it since she had all that success to maintain, and the marriage (not to mention the husband) was, to put it mildly, a disappointment. Since Rachel had always been the bright architect of her own success, she began to mull over the opposite. If she had what she had because she had earned it, what did that say about her bad marriage? She became consumed with the idea that she was a failure because she couldn't fix it, and although that didn't make any sense, it turns out that depression isn't really interested in logic.

The weight of it fell on her and drove her to her knees. Rachel remembers getting up in the morning (or not getting up, depending on how bad it had her that day) and trying to talk herself out of it. She gave herself stiff lectures that included phrases like "Buck up, lil' camper," but depression isn't a good listener, and the way she couldn't just "get over it" made her feel like even more of an abject loss. Pretty soon she was on leave from work, poking around home with an unemployed husband who clearly thought she should just pull herself together, being treated for her illness and trying really hard to just put one foot in front of the other. It was at the darkest time that, in a moment of prescience that makes perfect sense to me but was an enormous leap for Rachel, she got online and ordered a huge afghan pattern and an outstanding twenty-six balls of yarn to make it.

When I first heard about this, I thought the woman had just bought herself a one-way ticket to Make-It-Worse-If-You-Can Land. The last thing I thought Rachel needed was a huge undertaking. The last thing. People who feel hopeless, I thought, should be making mittens or hats or things that were done quickly so that they could get a sense of movement. An afghan the size of a small island? I wasn't so sure.

Rachel was, or maybe she wasn't, but when all those balls of double-knitting wool showed up, she got out her 3.75-mm needles and cast on. The pattern started with a smallish square of garter stitch, just about a foot across. When you had that done, you knit another square that attached to that one, then an even larger rectangle that spanned both the squares. If you got that far, then a fourth even larger rectangle went on at right angles to the first one, and so on and so on, until the last immense shape was the full length of the entire afghan and a couple of feet deep. Should you still have control of your faculties, or give a care about it in any way, you then picked up an enormous border around the entire thing and knit until you begged for mercy. Every stitch of the thing was a knit. No purls, no through was big. Really big. Completing a hat to give you confidence that someday you'll be joyful again is like throwing peanuts at a rhinoceros bearing down on you in the savanna and thinking you can take it down. Coming back from her dark place was slow and arduous, and like the blanket, it was taking months, and in that way, it was a good match. There were days, Rachel will tell you now, that all she did was work on that blanket. Days that she got up and couldn't face anything in the world at all. On those days she sat with that damned blanket, and she knit. Stitch after stitch, small accomplishment after small accomplishment. It didn't seem like much, a few rows on a behemoth of a thing, but it did make a difference. It added up. No matter how slowly the blanket was getting done, it was getting done. The blanket was undeniably slow movement, but it was absolutely forward movement, and it was resonant for Rachel. Even if she didn't feel better or look better, that blanket gave her the knowledge that it was possible to be better, a little at a time, even in the face of something that seemed surely insurmountable.

Months passed, and as they did, the squares got bigger. Not coincidentally, Rachel's ability to handle bigger things got bigger, too. She started turning up at the yarn shop more often. She helped stock books. She bought coffee. She laughed more often. There were starting to be times when she didn't just sit and knit like it was the only sure thing she could hold onto. Every day she worked on that blanket. Every day, she made some more forward movement. Progress was black and white while she was knitting. There was no way to be a failure. If she knit even one stitch, she was closer to done, and that was a grand and uplifting thing. Rachel knit on, and by the time she was picking up more than a thousand stitches around the edge of the ocean of garter stitch so she could knit even more garter stitch, I knew she was going to be all right. That much of an edge simply can't be attempted without a certain faith in yourself and your abilities.

Rachel finished the blanket one day while I wasn't there, and I'm sorry I missed the final moment. Legend has it that she sailed into the street outside the yarn shop with it furled out behind her like a cape and accosted another knitter in the road, just to share the glee. In what Rachel says is a remarkable coincidence, that day came at about the same time as she finally got the upper hand on depression. I'm not sure it's a coincidence at all. I'm not suggesting that major depression can be treated with knitting alone, nor am I implying that making a king-size garter stitch blanket could stand in the place of the very good drugs and therapy that Rachel also got, but I am saying this: I think she knit her way out of it. I think my funny, bright, vivacious, undeniably kind friend got a little lost. That the disease made her forget that if you get up in the morning and take care of your kid and are kind to yourself and your fellow humans, it's not possible to be a failure. I think her standards were too high for herself, and I think she lost track of what it felt to move forward, to accomplish things, and to be competent, and I think that knitting two full and undeniable miles of garter stitch gave it right back to her. That's what I think.

Dear Stephanie,

As I mentioned in my previous letter, Winterwool sport weight has definitely been discontinued. We understand that this has caused you some inconvenience, but yes, we are really sure it is unavailable. Please accept the enclosed coupon for 10% off of the worsted weight with our regrets.

Sincerely,
Robert
Customer Service Representative
Winterwool Inc.

Dear Stephanie,

Thank you for your response to my last letter. I'm very sorry that you have three quarters of a sweater knit out of that yarn, but that doesn't change the fact that we no longer sell this product. I understand that you feel entitled to "some sort of explanation" for our "irresponsible decision making," but there was simply no demand for the product.

In the future, since our product line can change without warning, we suggest that you purchase sufficient yarn to complete your project.

Regretfully,
Robert
Customer Service Representative
Winterwool Inc.

Dear Ms. Pearl-McPhee,

I regret my unfortunate choice of words in my last communication with you. Clearly I misspoke when I said that there was no demand for this yarn. I disagree with your base premise that there has to be some of this yarn somewhere in this place and assure you that our warehouse is a tidy and organized unit. There is no point in me acting on your suggestion to go down to the warehouse personally to conduct a search. Furthermore, I feel I must defend the company somewhat from your statement that this occurred right out of the blue. The product was discontinued almost nine months ago, and the color you're seeking was discontinued almost two years ago. Perhaps in the future you could look into starting a project right away so that any shortfalls have a better chance of being spotted before they become so obviously painful for you.

I assure you we are not "holding back on the goods" so that we can have it all for our "private stash." We are a yarn company; our goal is to get yarn out of here, not keep it in. Heck, I'm not even a knitter.

Apologetically,
Robert
Customer Service Representative
Winterwool Inc.

Dear Ms. Pearl-McPhee,

As a customer service professional, I don't think that if I were a knitter I would better understand what you're going through, and I think your insinuation that I do not care one little bit that Christmas is coming and there's no way that you'll have time to make a different sweater before then is "way off." From your choice language I can tell that this situation (for which Winterwool Inc. cannot be held responsible) is upsetting you a great deal. I have checked with the pattern support department to see "what the hell" you're supposed to do, and it is their suggestion that you make the sweater into a vest, as there should be adequate product to complete one. This seems to me a reasonable solution. I hope it helps. Regarding the second point in your most recent letter, I have to tell you that your suggestion that the company attempt to contact knitters to warn them of the impending discontinuation of product lines is a little far-fetched and nothing at all like the tornado early warning system, even if we did list it in the newspaper. I will, however, direct your idea to the appropriate departments, just the moment I have a minute.

Thank you,
Robert
Customer Service Representative
Winterwool Inc.

P.S.: No, I don't think that it is a brutal irony that our slogan is "Working to please knitters."

Madam,

I regret that there is no further action I can take to assist you in this matter, although I do feel badly that your husband dislikes vests so intensely. I personally have nothing against them. I will pass along to the pattern department your disappointment that this was the best they could manage and report your belief that you wouldn't have run out of yarn in the first place if they hadn't calculated yardage, as you so eloquently claimed, "like a six-year-old with a broken calculator." I assure you that there is no yarn here that will help you, and I can give you my full and personal promise that the answer would not be any different if you came down here, as you suggested, to personally conduct a search for the "two measly skeins" that you need to finish. There is no more. There has not been any for a long time, and there is nothing that any department here at Winterwool Inc. can do to assist you in this matter, even if you do talk to my mother. I think that you may have an easier time learning to live with this if we no longer communicate and end this difficult chapter of your life.

Robert
Customer Service Representative
Winterwool Inc.

Madam,

Although my position that nothing further can be done to help you locate further quantities of Winterwool has not changed, I did not want to leave your fourteen messages from Tuesday unanswered. I do understand the purpose of customer service, and I am sorry you feel that I do not. I must insist that you leave the level of my education out of this dispute, and I do not need to know how much you spend on wool each year, although if the figure you left on my answering machine at home (how did you get that number?) is correct, I would hazard a guess that you have problems that do not include a shortage of wool, although if true, it may explain why you think we are hoarding it. Please stop calling me, and for the love of God, walk away from the sweater. It's just not worth it.

Robert
Customer Service Representative
Winterwool Inc.

Things Crappy Yarn Taught Me

Woody Allen said, "Money is better than poverty, if only for financial reasons."

I have, for most of my knitting life, been a knitter with no money. I know that sounds a smidge dramatic, and I want to stress the difference—or at least the difference in my head—between a person with no money and a knitter with no money. A person who has no money might be looking for innovative ways to use a cardboard box for adequate housing, whereas a knitter with no money is looking for innovative ways to get knitting stuff. I wasn't starving or homeless, and I had money for a home much, much better than a cardboard box, and I certainly had food (though there were some memorable plain-pasta-with-margarine-sauce meals toward the end of a student loan or two), but I was a knitter with no yarn money.

At the beginning of my knitting poverty I was a student, and I lacked knitting experience as much as cold cash. I solved the issue by knitting with the absolutely cheapest yarn I could find. I went to discount stores and bought huge balls of appalling yarn with no regard for what it was made of or whether it possessed any quality that I might want in a finished project. I didn't worry about mundane things like whether the yarn I had chosen was stretchy enough for cables or fine enough for lace. I didn't worry that you couldn't block a plastic yarn, and I had chosen a pattern than needed blocking. I didn't worry about anything, not just out of ignorance but because there was no point. The reality was that I could buy only yarn that cost a dollar a pound. Introspection or investigation was pointless, since there were no options. Finding out that there were better things I couldn't afford was only going to be painful.

There were yarn shops in my neighborhood, and I peeked in them occasionally, but the prices (which I now think of as quite reasonable) were so far out of my reach that not only was it a joke to think about buying it, but I couldn't even imagine anyone taking that much money out of their budget to knit with the yarns I saw there. I wondered how the yarn shops stayed in business. I mean, could there really be enough knitters with more money than sense to support them? I may have even made fun of the fools who bought that stuff. (Considering my current stash, I sometimes wonder whether I permanently damaged my Karma with that. I half expected to get struck by lightning the first time I bought cashmere.)

During this period the yarn I bought was invariably acrylic, and this was more than twenty years ago. Acrylic in general was a shameful thing to do to a petrochemical, and I was buying the cheapest choice I could find, and generally speaking, the rule with yarn is the same as everything else. Except for good deals and good luck, you get what you pay for, and quality follows cash.

During these discount store scouring days, people didn't exactly clamor to get on my knitting gift list. Why on Earth I thought that if I bought awful yarn I would get great sweaters, I really don't know. I was experienced enough to grasp that if I bought rotten apples I couldn't have good applesauce, but I think that I was tricked by the way that knitting is an act of transformation. I was already turning yarn into something else, and I think that meant that I really believed that I could turn crap into good stuff. When things turned out crappy, and there were some unbelievably crappy things knit by me during that time, things that live in family legend and are still spoken of at family gatherings, I thought that it was my skills that made my finished projects nasty or stiff, wear poorly, or stretch out of shape. I knit along, trying to turn straw into gold, and I failed miserably most of the time.

Over and over I was struck with what seemed to be totally random disasters. My grandmother (who invested time and money in her knitting) had given me an old pattern book that had a baby blanket in it. Knit lace, executed in a fine and almost transparent British wool. Lacking the resources to buy the yarn recommended (and smart enough not to get sucked into buying something so clearly unnecessary), I had gone to the discount store and bought a bag of acrylic mill ends that I thought would work. The balls and half balls of yellowy-white acrylic were packaged in a clear garbage bag (that should have been a tip-off for me, but I was young and that gave me false confidence), and I hugged the huge bag all the way home. It was about $3 for a blanket's worth. I thought I was a genius. $3! I was giddy with my thrifty glee.

The problems started immediately. First, there was the issue of density. Since the yarn recommended was lofty and delicate wool, and my yarn was extruded plastic, my version was sort of heavy, in the same way that Dolly Parton's hair was sort of big in the '80s. I did not let this deter me. There was also a problem trying to work the instruction "Pass slipped stitch over" in a yarn with no stretch at all. When I managed to yank the stitches over to where they should be, they stayed there, gaping rudely instead of snugging back like a more elastic yarn would. I didn't let this deter me either.

In addition, because I was knitting lace, the whole thing looked like the bricks of ramen noodles you buy at four for a dollar. (I was well acquainted with these.) I phoned my grandmother and told her that my stitches weren't nice, and my work didn't lie flat like the picture. "Block it," she mandated. "Blocking evens out your work and stretches lace to open it up." I looked up *blocking* in my book and followed the directions. The book and my grandmother both agreed that blocking made knitting "flat and even." (The book and my grandmother also probably agreed that all bets were off if you were knitting with discount mill ends, but they didn't say so.) I followed instructions, wetting and pinning out my work, but (probably because I was trying to block the yarn equivalent of a waterproof sailing rope) the knitting didn't respond the way the book said it would. I still remember the tragic confusion I felt when I took the pins out of my beautiful lace blanket, and as my hours and hours of work were released from the tension, it sprang back to its original form. It was still rippling and twisted, the stitches still gaped, and frankly, it still looked like crap.

In a monumental moment of formidable stupidity (though at the time it felt like ingenuity, and it would have been if it had worked), I tried to counter these problems in a new way. I swear now, as I swore to my mother then, while trying desperately to peel, scrape, and otherwise scour the layer of blackened plastic goo off of her iron while I sobbed and the acrid scent of scorched acrylic filled the air, that it had never, ever occurred to me that a yarn could melt. The blanket was entirely ruined.

After that I got a pretty good job, and things improved fast. I invested in better yarn, patterns, and tools, and lo and behold, the stuff I was making started looking better, too. Julia Child said that you should cook with the best ingredients you can afford, and my own mother told me that you can't turn a sow's ear into a silk purse, but I had no idea what good materials could do to produce good knitted stuff. Suddenly the sweaters were soft, light, warm, and elastic. Shawls stayed blocked, mittens felted slightly in a bath and became warmer and warmer with wearing. My knitting needles were a pleasure to work with, my knitting basket overflowed with success and joy. I was in heaven. I was now a regular at the yarn shop, and I took back everything I had ever said about people who wasted their money on wool. (I now mocked people who bought sweaters.) I was enlightened. Good yarn was a pleasure all by itself.

Enter my first baby a few years later, and exit the whole yarn budget. All of it. I was right back to only affording crap, and not much of it, but something had happened. I had staggered back into the discount store, picked up a big ball of yarn that I had happily knit for years, and noticed that it was crap. I'd gotten a taste for the good stuff, and there was no way I was going backward. Now I had a problem, though. I wanted only the good stuff, but I still didn't have any money to buy it with. I could really afford only yarn that cost less than carrots, and short of selling the baby, which though lucrative had obvious moral problems, I was screwed. This time, though, I got to thinking creatively, and I found that with ingenuity, focus, and the sort of clear reasoning one usually associates with nuclear physics rather than knitting, I could knit with the best of them. I recycled yarn from thrift store sweaters, I offered to knit yarn shop samples in exchange for store credit, I put out the word that I accepted yarn orphans happily, and when Christmas or my birthday came, I wanted only one thing. It worked out, and three babies (and ten years) later it got easier.

Nowadays, I have what my younger self would think was an outrageous yarn budget. If the nineteen-year-old me bumped into the forty-year-old me, she would probably make fun of her. (I suppose nineteen-year-olds mock forty-year-olds a fair bit anyway, but you see my point, I'm sure.) In my grown-up, got-a-job reality, I still can't haul off and buy exactly what I want or as much as I want, and I still avoid making direct contact with cashmere at the yarn shop in case it weakens me, but mostly I can have what I want if I'm smart about the budget or save up for a while or something.

Sometimes, though, when I see a young knitter, nestled among my friends in the yarn shop, a knitter who somehow reminds me of me at that age, a knitter who's young and broke and expertly cabling an intricate sweater made of absolutely crappy yarn or constructing a baby blanket that could be nothing short of a personal legacy, were she not knitting it out of yarn that will be one of the only things that survives the apocalypse, sometimes I still want to rescue her. I want to go up to her and say, "You're a fantastic knitter. I can see that. I can tell you're destined for knitterly greatness, so please believe me when I tell you this: Your talent is not enough. You are not going to be able to rise above that yarn. You are going to be great, but that yarn is crap, and no amount of your formidable skill is going to change that." And then, in this fantasy, I pull out a big bag of decent yarn from my stash, and I press it into her hands with a fervor, and I tell her, "Here. Take this. It's not the best that there is, but it's better than what you're using by a lot. I've got a lot more, and I just want you to have this so that you can see what's possible," and in that crazy place in my head, she doesn't run screaming away from me, or look at me the way other people do when I love yarn more than society suggests is appropriate. No, no, in this daydream, she takes a little out of the bag and holds it in her hands, and turns it over, feeling the difference that a little money makes. Maybe she casts on, and as she does, her face fills with a light and a joy that tells me that she totally gets it, she totally understands that if you start with junk you end up with junk and that having this means that she's not going to make junk anymore, even though she's really talented. I lift a veil

It's about Balance

Yarn shops make me nervous.

Don't get me wrong, I love them. I feel like I belong in them, and I almost always feel welcome in them. I find yarn-shop owners pretty universally kind, or if not kind, at the very least quite predictable. I've been in hundreds of shops, being the traveling knitter that I am, and I find it very reassuring that yarn shops are the same all over. Yarn, patterns, needles, hooks, and me giving them all my money.

That's why they make me nervous. When I'm in a yarn shop, I know that I am vulnerable. Weakened. I don't know whether it's just the logical negative consequence of being surrounded by that much of your favorite stuff, I don't know whether it's the giddiness induced by that much possibility in one place. I've even supposed that it could be a chemical reaction, that after this many years I've become sensitized to the wool fumes or the glue on ball bands, but I can tell you that every single minute I'm in a yarn shop I know that I'm just one "here, feel this" away from a trunkload of alpaca, an empty bank account, and a dirty feeling. I have virtually no defenses against yarn, and so while I'm in there, I try not to let my guard down. I try to be aware of the subtle marketing ploys yarn shops use against me, things like placing little impulse items by the cash register, or putting the cashmere by the half-price sock yarn to lure you into its sphere of influence. I attempt to remain aware that the shop owner and employees are particularly dangerous. I love them, I feel welcome and cherished by them, but I also know that I am a vital part of their business plan, and a weak knitter like me might as well have a sign stapled to me that says, "I will give you all my grocery money if you show me the merino."

Knowing that this is the reality, I try to keep my wits about me, and trying to maintain alertness only makes me more nervous. Once I'm alert I start worrying about being too defensive, and that leads straight to a concern that I'll offend them by avoiding their ploys, and once I'm upset about trying not to offend the shop owner, I slide all the way to a little weird and jumpy. Once I know I'm being weird and jumpy, I try not to be worried about that, and by then I'm so nervous that I do the only reasonable thing, which is to fold like a deck of cards, buy seventeen skeins of sock yarn, and get the hell out.

Now, I know that this is unreasonable, and I'm eternally grateful that yarn shop owners can't seem to tell that I'm freaked out (or are at least pretending they don't notice and have agreed on a store policy that involves approaching me with some caution). I'd love to come to grips with my nature and learn to relax around wool for sale, but as long as it has the upper hand this way, I'm bound to make mistakes.

The fact that I am certain to make these mistakes compounds the problem, because I've never been the sort of person who knows how to recover from a mistake. I always know that there's a simple way out of what's gone wrong, but at the time it never seems like the right thing to do, or I don't think of the simple, obvious solution until after I've gotten through it in some other, less graceful way, figuring out the perfect way my accidentally odd behavior should have been handled four hours later when I'm at home. I know that if a sweater kit gets the better of me and I enter the yarn-store shame spiral and find myself standing outside the shop in the cold hard light of day with a pattern for a sweater I'll never knit and seventeen skeins of yarn in a color that, now that I have a little distance from the store, I suddenly understand will make me look both anemic and jaundiced, the simple thing to do, finding myself having fallen down that way, is to breathe a little fresh air and then go back in and say, "I'm terribly sorry. I don't know what happened there. I got carried away and, darn it, I don't want this, and I'd like to return it," but I can't. I worry I'll look stupid or, because so much of my business life is wrapped up in knitting, that I might look unprofessional. (Somehow, I don't worry that it looks sort of stupid that I just bought the ugly yarn she's been trying to unload for seven years.) I worry that they'll take my moment of clarity the wrong way and that I'll hurt their feelings or offend them by bringing them back their beloved yarn. In the absence of a truly safe course of action, I always do the same thing. I go home, put the yarn in the stash, and stare at it for nineteen years until I can't stand it anymore and give it away. (Nobody said it was a good system. Just a system.)

I've tried to find good ways out of bad mistakes ever since, but the lingering knowledge that I don't really think fast when I've made a mistake has stayed with me, and it only makes me more nervous when I'm in a situation where I might make a mistake, which only makes a mistake more likely, which in turn makes me more nervous. (It's a terrible loop.)

Such was my mood in a yarn shop not too long ago. It was reasonably new, and I'd been in there only once before, and both times the place was empty. The charming owner was being very welcoming and clearly wanted my financial support, and I liked her a lot and wanted to support her endeavor. Since the best thing you can do to please and support a yarn-shop owner is to buy yarn, I had been perusing the store for a while, trying to find something I wanted. I was there with my yarn budget for the month, determined to spend it, and I was getting increasingly nervous. I didn't want to hurt her feelings by not buying something, but what she had really wasn't to my taste. Once I got nervous and started worrying, my fate was sealed. I felt the familiar fear, and I know I don't think well under those circumstances, so I decided to try and get out before I attempted to explain how surprised I was that she had achieved the near miracle of buying an entire inventory of yarn that I hated, so I grabbed the only thing I almost liked in the whole shop and went to the cash register, doing what I always did when I was up against the wall. Me and the yarn, forking over a credit card, feeling some relief about how well I was doing. I hadn't done anything strange or said anything strange, I hadn't accidentally insulted her, and as far as

I knew I didn't have toilet paper stuck to my shoe. I was thinking it was all coming off so well that I was actually starting to think there was no reason to be nervous, when it all came crashing down.

The owner asked for my name, and I gave it to her. She typed it into her shop computer, and since I'd been in there once before, my customer profile came up on the screen facing her. As the owner looked from the screen to the yarn, then back to the screen again, it all started coming back to me.

"Oh," the owner said, looking unexpectedly nervous herself, "funny you're buying this kit. Didn't you buy it the last time you were in?" And I knew it was true. Damn it. I was caught in the headlights again. If she'd just said, "Hey, you already bought this," if it had been stated as a fact, then maybe I would have done the right thing. Maybe then I would have looked at her and said, "Oh, silly me," and gotten away, but she didn't. She had asked me whether I had it (even though she could see right on that screen that I did), and somehow, just like always, I inexplicably couldn't face up to it. I couldn't open my mouth and say it. I should have said, "Oh, yeah, I did, but I love it so much that I wanted a second one." That would have been fine. Perfectly acceptable. She would have been complimented, I could have still given her the money. It was elegant and perfect, and somehow none of those possibilities occurred to me. Instead I looked right at her, set my feet squarely, and said, "Nope."

A confused expression flickered on her face; she glanced back at that screen and said, "Are you sure? If you have a big stash. . . ."

I cursed her. Why didn't she just say it? Why didn't she just say,

"Hey, guess what. You're wrong. It says right here that every time you come in the shop you've bought the same thing. You have this. At least go get another color." But she didn't. She left room for the charade to continue, and it did. I knew she knew, I think she knew I knew, but I was committed to the process of screwing this up, and every moment that passed only got me deeper in and further from an out. I knew this. I knew it was just like running down the road because I didn't want to be embarrassed, in the process working all the way up from a small embarrassment to a freakshow humiliation. I was helpless to stop it. I looked at her again and said, "No, I'm sure. I didn't buy this kit before," and I tried to smile warmly and probably pulled off an odd grimace. Just ring it up, I thought. Just do it. Just end it for both of us, and I'll leave and stand in the driveway and think of all the ways I could have done this better, and you can call all your friends and tell them that Stephanie Pearl-McPhee was just in the shop, and boy is she weird. Let's just get it done.

"Alright," she said slowly.

"Alright," I said firmly. She rang it up. I gave her the money, thanked her warmly for her time, and attempted to walk off confidently. That would have gone better had I not tripped on the mat at the door.

Outside, I moved to where she couldn't see me and looked at the yarn. Damn it. Like I don't have a big enough stash without buying the same thing twice.

I looked at that yarn and I looked down the street. I'm surprised I didn't see Julie.

A Knitter's Sense of Snow

Like that of most Canadian children, Abby's childhood memories were chock full of experiences of every possible kind of snow. There was the packing snow that was dense, wet, and heavy and made the most excellent igloos, snowballs, and snowmen. There was the high holy snow of childhood, the snow that falls in huge quantities, all rushing in through the nighttime. Abby could remember lying in bed as a little girl, watching the snow fall by the street lamps, hoping that when she woke up in the morning there would be the insulated quiet and crazy luminous light that might mean it was a snow day. She could recall dreading the walk to school on days the sky had rained the smallest accumulated diamonds, tiny adamantine snow that glittered and squeaked tellingly underfoot. That noise, kids were taught in school, is a way of telling the temperature. Snow only squeaks that way if the snow is less than 14°F, and that sound has come to be the sound that cold makes, as far as Abby was concerned. Snowscrunch. Now that she was a grown-up, Abby was most likely

Come to think of it, there was the day on the way back from the grocery store, too. The kids were all little, and Abby ran out of something critical during a blizzard and was forced to bundle up all three of them and go out into the snow. What was it? Bread? Milk? For the life of her she couldn't recall what started the episode. It hardly mattered, either, for the horror was in how it ended. After taking forever to get the kids into their snow stuff and out of the apartment, she had an irritable preschooler, a biting toddler, and a screaming baby, and things only went from bad to worse. There was deterioration as they trudged through the snow to the store, further decline in the store as everybody got hot and sweaty from wearing snowgear inside, and everyone started screaming. The epic ended on the way home as Abby tried to hold it together, with the baby in the sling and the toddler in the stroller and the groceries over her arm and the preschooler standing in a snowbank up to her armpits crying about being stuck and buried, when Abby reached down inside herself for whatever strength mothers find when things are that bad, and she found it. She hauled the kid out of that snowbank, hiked the baby up on her hip, squinted into the swirling snow, and heaved that stroller forward, damn it. Abby still thought that she had never been the same after what happened next . . . which was that one whole wheel snapped off of the stroller in the snow, and all four of them fell down into that treacherous white. Groceries, broken stroller, preschooler, toddler, baby, all of them sodden, everything smashed or squashed, all of them crying in the snow. Abby didn't even have a clear memory of how she got them all home after that, a reaction she thought might be post-traumatic stress disorder.

Then there was the way the older she got, the harder it became to make a snowman taller than you. (If you can't make a snowman taller than you, then what's the point?) The way that people stopped paying her to shovel the driveway once she owned the driveway . . . and just somehow, the way that as a grownup, snow had started to seem like an impediment. Abby knit and thought about all of that as she watched the snow fall outside, watched the wind push it into drifts. She sipped her tea and felt a pang of fondness for snow, and she decided. She was going to take it back. Abby wasn't going to let becoming a grownup ruin her sense of snow. She would wait for the perfect snow, and she would reclaim the joy that was in it. She might even knit some perfect mittens while she waited for it.

It didn't take long at all for the perfect snow to come. Abby knew it when she saw it start one afternoon. The snow fell and fell and fell. It was big fluffy flakes, the ones that are bigger than snowflakes should ever properly be, the ones that are a million snowflakes clumped together on the way down. When you see those, you know it's not too cold. She watched it accumulate quickly on the road and side-walk. When you see that, you know it's not too warm. Flakes like those, they would be packing snow. If they were sticking to themselves on the way down, then they would stick to themselves in snowballs, on hills. It was perfect snow for her purposes, and it just kept drift-ing down.

What her purposes were, that remained to be seen. Abby decided just to go out and enjoy the snow. Just walk around in it and look at it from the outside instead of the inside and see what happened, and being a knitter paid off. Abby donned her cabled hat and her warm Fair Isle mittens, even wound her alpaca scarf around her neck. She was walking in the snow, and it wasn't cold at all, and she reflected on how this was really where a knitter should be. Out in the snow, using the things she'd knit. Knitters should be embracing the cold that motivated them to turn out these things in the first place. What was the point of waging a personal war against chilliness if you never went into the snow to reap the rewards? As she walked, Abby lifted her hands and turned her mittened palms over to catch snowflakes, then squinted at them sparkling in the dark. The world was so quiet while it was snowing, and she stood and tried to hear the sound it made falling, thinking maybe that so much snow falling at once just had to make a noise. It didn't, but as Abby stood there in the dark, watching each branch get its own little hat of white, she felt more and more joyful, and she had an idea.

By the time she got to the toboggan hill where her daughter had gone with her friends, the thrill of snow hadn't lifted at all and Abby was even warmer, partly because of her alpaca and her excitement, and partly because hiking up a snow-covered hill in a blizzard was a little harder in her forties than she remembered. In fact, her daughter Rose and her buddies had made two full circuits up and down the hill in the time that it took her to ascend to the summit. Rose saw her mum arrive and raised a suspicious eyebrow at her, but once she worked out that Abby wasn't there because she was in any sort of trouble, she decided to deal with the horror of her mother appearing in public by ignoring her entirely.

Standing there, Abby looked around and watched the kids play in the snow, and in a fit of she didn't quite know what, Abby tipped her head back, toward the sky and stars. She closed her eyes, and the snowflakes fell on her lids and face, tiny, perfect pinpoints of exquisite cold. They began to collect in her eyelashes and, following some romantic urge, she opened her mouth and stuck out her tongue. There she stood, in the dark, on the top of a hill, forgetting that there was probably acid snow or pollution or some good reason not to eat snow, even snow that wasn't yellow, and she let it fall. It was spectacular.

It was also, apparently, embarrassing and Rose, mortified in all the ways that only a thirteen-year-old can be when her mother is being obviously weird in public, came over and elbowed her hard to bring her back.

"Mum," Rose whispered, "Stop it. Why are you here? Why are you doing that? Is something wrong with your face?" Abby looked at the kid, and for a moment she regretted invading Rose's fun before she remembered that she was there to capture her childlike whimsy for snow, and darn it all, no child was going to get in the way of that.

"Don't badger me, Rose," Abby said. "I'm just enjoying the snow."

"Do you have to enjoy it here?" her daughter asked, looking nervously over her shoulder at her friends. There's a social contract in place that doesn't allow mothers to hang out with kids, and she wondered how long her mum could break it before her friends would leave. "You know, it's snowing all over the city."

"No badgering," her mum replied, and she watched some of her daughter's young friends fly down the hill on a wooden toboggan.

The kids were moving so fast one of them had her hat blown off. They whooped and screamed as the group hit a wee bump and the toboggan slowly came to a stop at the bottom of the hill, and all the girls tumbled off, giggling in a heap.

"Rose?" Abby said, turning to face her daughter, looking as stern and powerful as possible, since her idea wasn't going to go over well at all, "I'm going to need to borrow a toboggan."

In Toronto, trees near the bottoms of hills in wintertime are nothing more than accidents waiting to happen, and every fall the city comes around with mountains of old tires that they put around the trunks to serve as bumpers for sledding kids. (I guess the city worked out that providing this service was infinitely cheaper than the alternative, which would only begin with a fleet of ambulances.) Abby, who had always thought this was a very good idea, reflected now, as she sat at the top of the hill on a borrowed toboggan, that it was nothing short of bloody brilliant. She'd been sitting there a while, since it takes real time to stuff adult concern for life into a back pocket, and the gaggle of thirteen- and fourteen-year-olds milling around anxiously behind her were growing more and more concerned about her behavior. Abby could feel the pressure, knew that she was killing Rose, and took a deep breath, bent her knees, leaned back to get a good launch position, and . . . sat there.

Rose watched this whole thing, desperate to get her mother moving along and beginning to imagine that this series of false starts might be becoming a habit. The idea that her mum could be here a while was too awful to imagine, and so she approached.

"Mum? You've been sitting there a while. Your bum is getting wet, and nobody is tobogganing. We're waiting for you. You're on our toboggan." Then she waited. Nothing happened, and Rose wondered whether maybe her mother was waiting for some sort of permission.

"It's your turn," she said. Abby didn't move. Sure, she thought about moving, and if Rose could have seen inside her mother's head she would have been impressed with the progress she was making toward moving, but outwardly it looked for all the world like Abby was just sitting on a sled at the top of a hill. Eyes fixed ahead, snow falling on her handknit hat.

Rose shifted her weight from foot to foot. She glanced behind her and shrugged at the questions in her friends' eyes. She didn't know why her mum didn't go. In a moment that would have made her mother proud, had she known it had occurred, Rose decided not to push her mum squarely in the back and end this thing. Instead, she leaned forward again. "Are you scared?" Abby looked gratefully at her daughter and thought about saying, "Hell, yes," and she thought about asking Rose to push her squarely in the back.

"Mum," whispered Rose. "Sometimes you just have to do it. Going down is better than going home. Everybody is watching, and those are your only two choices. Do you want to go home?"

Abby looked at her very wise daughter, and she knew that it was entirely true; she knew that the only thing that could be worse than ending up a mangled heap at the bottom of a snowhill in Toronto was getting off that toboggan and kissing the experience good-bye forever. Abby took another deep breath. "Screw it," she thought.

She thought about being eighty years old and looking back on her life and decided she wanted to remember a day when in her forties, she'd tossed herself down a hill like a kid again, not a day where she humiliated herself in front of a group of teenagers by being afraid. Besides, these kids had been throwing themselves down the hill all day and nothing had happened to them. Adult cowardice was not going to get her, damn it all. It was just snow, just a toboggan. Abby blinked, set her jaw, and bent her knees. Rose looked hopeful. She asked whether Abby wanted a push. Abby resisted the urge to push Rose (good parenting is all about what you *don't* do most days) and instead muttered, "Don't badger me, Rose. I'm going; I'm going when I'm ready." And then suddenly, she was ready.

Abby pulled her scarf up over her mouth and nose like an Olympic downhill skier adjusts her mask. She wished briefly for a helmet but realized that concerns about safety and brain injuries were the kind of silly adult overthinking that kept grownups from having any fun.

She bent her knees again, and this time she pulled her feet into the sled behind the curl of the bow and grasped the ropes. The sled was already beginning to inch down the hill, and Abby leaned forward, making herself low, lean, and fast, and the sled picked up speed. It was glorious. The snow was still falling, and as she began to whoosh down the hill (it really was a big hill, especially now that she was going down it this fast) she remembered everything about loving this. The snow hit her softly in the face, making her feel like a speeding train. The toboggan skimmed the snowy earth faster and faster, little bumps and swells adding thrill to the ride. Abby began to laugh. The toboggan went faster. Abby remembered what it was like to be out of control and to give in to the youthful urge for speed and irresponsibility. She remembered the thrill of doing something that felt wildly dangerous (even though it was mostly safe), reveled in joyous risk taking, and wondered briefly (because she was really going fast now, almost scary fast) whether people would still do drugs or have road rage if you could get a snowhill into every neighborhood year-round. Squinting into the snow as the toboggan shot down the hill at a phenomenal speed, Abby was being jostled around on the toboggan as she gripped the sled string as hard as she could, as though a grip on a string would make any difference at all; she remembered all of this as a dark object appeared through the snow in front of her.

Suddenly, the kids huddled at the top of the hill were shouting. From behind her, Abby heard the screaming start. "Left, left!," some shrieked. "Right, go right!," called others, and a few of the voices simply bellowed, "Turn!" or "Treeeeee!"

For one horrible moment as the tree swelled ever larger and faster in front of her, Abby tried to do all of those things. Go left, go right, turn, anything to go around the tree. She panicked and pulled back on the sled rope threaded through the front of the toboggan, instinctively trying to whoa the curved wooden harbinger of death, but as any twelve-year-old can tell you, toboggans are not horses, and pulling on the rope raises the nose of the sled and, as Abby discovered, speeds up the thing. Abby could scarcely breathe now. The kids were still yelling, "Turn, turn!" and now Rose was yelling,

"Mum, Mum!" and Abby was absolutely going to hit the tree. Absolutely. From the very back of her mind she pulled up a memory, a memory of four girls on a toboggan, careening wildly down a hill and one of them calling "left" and all four girls leaning left on the toboggan, left hands dragging in the snow as the sled pulled left. Noting her proximity to the tree (and imagining the moment on the way to the hospital when Rose said, "Why didn't you just lean to turn it?"), Abby offered a quick thanks to the City of Toronto for the tires around the bottom of the tree that meant she wasn't about to hit a seriously hard object, just a firm one, extended her hand to the left to drag like a rudder, and leaned her weight over that way.

Despite what happened next, Abby would swear for the rest of her life that it should have worked. Abby would tell you that she was positive that you could turn a toboggan by shifting your weight and dragging your hand in the snow, that what had happened that day on the hill had nothing at all to do with the plan or the correctness of her idea. She would shake her head a little at parties where her husband or her kids told the story of the toboggan ride and how it ended that day and insist (sometimes a little angrily) that it had been conspiracy and coincidence that had made it end the way that it did—certainly not incompetence. She swore nobody would have been able to make something different happen, that the ending had been ordained by the fates the minute she put her bum on that sled. The minute she headed down the hill, a chain of events that she was helpless to change had begun to unfold. She swore, in short, that what had happened wasn't her fault.

What happened then was that as Abby (who, for the record, is absolutely right, dragging your hand like a rudder and shifting your weight definitely does turn a speeding toboggan) leaned over to the left and began to drag that hand in the snow, the toboggan hit a bump. It was a very little bump, hardly anything at all that would have bothered her had she not begun her plan, but she had begun, and that little bump transferred through her body and, shifted as she was to the left, whacked her left hand more firmly on the ground than she had intended. Abby's hand caught in the deep snow for just one second, and as it did Abby was suddenly and completely struck with the realization that she was screwed. The moment that her hand was caught was just long enough (it doesn't take long for things to happen, Abby thought later, when you are going that fast) to pull her off the sled, and she fell to the left. She felt her bottom part company with the sled, felt it come away, and through the cloud of swirling snow hitting her in the face she watched it slide toward the tree. Clawing at the snow, trying to stop her own mad slide, Abby watched the toboggan coast toward the tree, losing speed fast now that it wasn't carrying a middle-aged woman to her death, and then gently hit the tree and come to a rest on its side, bottom leaning against the tires around the trunk.

Abby saw this, the sled leaning up against the tires like that, and she felt what can only be described as deep regret. What she realized as she continued to pick up speed was that she had found the only possible way on a toboggan hill in the city of Toronto, where the trees are wrapped with tires just so that you can't hit something really hard going really fast, to do exactly that anyway.

The precise moment that Abby hit the sled against the tires against the tree with the full force of her body is best not described in detail, nor is it a moment that Abby cares to discuss. All she will tell you, if you ask her, is that she hit that sled so hard that the remarkable consequence was not pain (although there was a great deal of pain) but the spectacular explosion of colors. Abby hit that tree so hard that the little audience of teenagers standing at the top of the hill, help- less to stop the collision from happening and really hoping that she didn't get killed or break the toboggan so they couldn't have a turn, all flinched and gasped and made the same noise that everybody makes at the theater when a character is abruptly mauled by a zombie.

For a time after that, everything was quiet. The kids stood silently in the snow, peering down the hill at Abby's body lying at the foot of the tree, and they held their breath and watched for signs of life. Abby, far away at the bottom of the hill, was quiet, too, having had not just the air but all thought smashed right out of her. She rolled onto her back (bringing a collective sigh of relief from the assembled masses, who really didn't want to have to figure out what to do with someone's dead mother) and let the snow fall on her face. She opened her eyes and looked up, watching the snow come out of the sky far above her and drift beautifully down from straight above. Abby lay there, feeling the snow underneath her begin to melt through the full length of her jeans, and she began to form two thoughts: first, that episodes like this were probably part of the reason that the other mothers didn't want her on committees; and second, that she hoped to hell that none of those kids had a cameraphone.

It was the second thought that got her half-upright, plunked awkwardly in the drift of snow, checking herself over for injuries as Rose came skidding down the hill, coming to a scurrying halt by her snow-covered mother, and she opened her mouth to say something and then closed it again. Abby stared at her, the snow on her face melting and dripping into her eyes, and she waited. In that moment, Rose saw that look in her mother's eyes, and for the first time in her young life she got it.

"Mummy?" Rose inquired, as respectfully as she ever had, heaven bless her, "I'm not badgering, but would you like to go home . . . now?"

Abby did. She limped along home in the very pretty, very perfect snow, and she had a hot bath and got a cup of tea and her knitting. Turns out she drew the right conclusions after all. Knitting while the snow falls. How very cozy.

CHAPTER 7

Cast Off

Stories of Ends, Giving Up, and
Living to Knit Another Day

Samantha

When Samantha knits, it astounds me. She's fourteen years old now, a pretty big girl, and when she picks up the needles to knit, she does so with a great deal of ease and a miraculous amount of assurance. Assurance and ease that you would expect from a confident and experienced knitter, not one who, like Sam, picks up the needles only a few times a year, if that.

Sam has always been like this. She is my baby, my youngest and last, and I knew she would be my last kick at the maternal can when she was born. This somehow filled me with a tenderness that I'm pretty sure my other kids didn't find in me. I'm sure Sam will be laughing when she reads this. Everyone will, as I am not known for my tenderness. Empathy, yes. Cleverness, sometimes. Wit, most days. Tenderness? No. I am simply not that sort of mother. I am the sort of mother who finds maternal sentiment vaguely nauseating, and a have never cut the crusts off anyone's sandwich. I am the sort of mother who never has a bandage, forgets the extra diapers, and makes up games like "how long can we go without talking?" or "let's pretend we're rocks!" just to get a moment's peace. When other mothers gushed about their feelings about their babies and the fulfillment they found in wiping noses and bottoms, I used to have to fake it a little to not get expelled from playgroup.

"Isn't it wonderful?" they would exclaim while adoringly stroking the cheek of their demon offspring, who had just pulled everything off all my bookcases and bitten my cat, and I would nod sagely, wondering when the hell naptime was and why I couldn't feel what they did. Motherhood was just so much work that I often failed to find any sentiments in it that you could write on a card. I loved my children, but I didn't see the romance in any job that had this much to do with this variety of bodily fluids. Right up until Sam. With Sam, everything suddenly had a sweetness to it that I hadn't been able to see through the daily slog of laundry, sliced apples, and parenting the other two. When she got me up in the dead of the night to nurse, I wasn't (as) frustrated. Sometimes all I could think of as we sat in the deep dark together was that this could be the last time I nursed a baby in the night, and then I would look down at Samantha's fingers curled like new leaves and her wee down of blondish hair and suddenly, and rather uncharacteristically, I wouldn't mind so much. Tenderness would wash over me, and the knowledge that I was going to stagger through the next day sleep deprived and maniacal with three sticky, messy kids who were totally teamed up against me and my desire for sanity and ten minutes with a book would fade, however temporarily.

Samantha has undeniably been the wrong kid to be on the receiving end of all this saccharine thinking, and this newfound tenderness and rampant desire to romanticize every moment of her childhood (the last time I'll potty train, the last time anyone will play with blocks) are something that, since she is a great deal like me, she has trouble dealing with. She's always been straightforward, clear thinking, and efficient, and here I am trying to draw hearts and flowers around all these moments of her youth. I'd watch her play, and tears would well up at "the last time anyone will eat a blue crayon," and Sam would look over, see me misting over, and give me right back a phrase I gave all the girls all the time: "Pull yourself together."

Sam learned to knit at about the same age as the other two, right around the time she learned to read, and she took to it like the other playgroup mothers took to making their own playdough. I showed her how, guiding her little girl fingers around wooden needles and real wool, and while I sighed and shed discreet tears over "the last first time one of my children would knit" she effortlessly integrated the skill, then put it down and went back to her coloring. It didn't surprise me that she was good at it. She'd done everything the same way. Samantha had never struggled with anything. She's a good learner, and whereas my other kids' growth had been marked by periods of instability, unsteadiness, and general incompetence due to youth and inexperience, Sam's wasn't. She didn't toddle drunkenly around the living room while she was learning to walk; she got up and went. As she grew, her ability to learn was matched by her sense of humor and frank confidence, and unlike my other girls, on the first day of school she marched smartly away from me, leaving me weeping in the schoolyard about "my baby" and "the last first day of school." (I recovered promptly, though, when I realized that I had three hours to go to the bathroom by myself and drink a whole cup of coffee that didn't have anything mysterious floating in it.) Given this nature, I wasn't at all surprised she was so good at knitting. It knocked the sense right off me that then she put it down and walked away.

When I learn to do something new, I undergo a period of profound interest (some might call it obsession, but I think that's a bit strong) in that new thing. When I learned to bake bread I could have run a bakery with all that I turned out, and there was a similar incident involving making my own marmalade. (By the way, if you'd like a jar, I still have plenty.) When I learned something new I celebrated by going to town with it. Not Sam. Learn it, know it, move on. The knitting was a perfect example, and one that was particularly hard for me to understand, considering that I've been celebrating learning to knit by doing it daily for thirty-five years. For the life of me, I cannot understand why Sam and I can't have this tender connection. She could be my "last knitting daughter." We could go to shops together and knit in the evenings; it would be wonderful and sentimental, and I would be able to score some points back on my motherhood scorecard. Maybe make up for the afternoon I told them all that Santa Claus was never coming back to the house again if they didn't let me have a bath alone. It would have been one thing if she sucked at it or found it difficult, but she was, and is, an entirely natural knitter.

Never Can Say Good-bye

As I stood in the garage, it all became so perfectly clear. After this many years together you want to believe that you are the ones who are going to make it, that you can beat the odds and stay together, but as I looked at my minivan hooked up to the mechanic's computer as if on life support, I knew.

In the beginning the van just seemed depressed. It leaked oil on the driveway. Then it was slow to start in the mornings, and it seemed a little sluggish when turning left. I accepted it. It's important to stay flexible in relationships. The van was aging, and old people and old things get quirky, and my van and I had been through a lot together, and if it needed a little compassion to grow old gracefully, I could stand by it. A suburban mother and her minivan are not easily parted; after all, it was only the van that stood between complete isolation and me. I was supportive of its needs. I thought about knitting it a cozy, or maybe a wheel cover. I wanted to cherish it in its golden years. The van and I were simply moving into the phase of a relationship where you stay together in spite of your quirks. I got self-help books from the library about working it out and changing my own oil, and I spent hours in the driveway with an oil pan and a good attitude. I thought about it while I knit.

Things got worse. The van started to make a disturbing noise and shudder while turning left. From time to time I feel the same way, so sympathetically, I adapted by planning right-turn-only routes and bargaining with the van. For my part, I agreed that I would knit in the van one evening a week while the kids were swimming. (I think he wanted more time together.) I would give it the premium gas, bury my building, hostile resentment, and never offend it by turning left, and in exchange it would start (most of the time). As I pored over the maps of my neighborhood at night, doing recon for my right-turn days, I wondered whether I was enabling the van. I felt a little like the van wasn't making an effort, but I was trying to stay together for the children, so I let it go.

The van and I were holding it together, but it took commitment. It's only three miles to the yarn shop, but with my right-turns-only-or-your-van-shudders system to spiral in ever-decreasing circles, it's a four-hour round trip. The strain was wearing me down. One afternoon, dizzy and exhausted with the children screaming things like "She's looking out my window" from the back seat, I got rattled, forgot myself, and attempted to turn left into the yarn shop.

The van instantly responded to the forbidden left turn by seizing, emitting a sound I could only compare to the noise of a large cat falling into a flushing toilet, and stopping dead mid-turn. Panic filled me, honking oncoming traffic squealed to a halt, and after four frantic attempts the van leaped back to life, lurched out of the intersection, and gracefully coasted into the yarn-shop parking lot, acting for all the world like nothing had just happened between us. I had to buy six skeins of the new merino sock yarn just to regain my composure.

When I came back to the van I sat in the driver's seat and thought about what had just happened. I realized that we needed professional help. The van was sick, and it had anger issues. It was time to let go of the shame of not being able to maintain my own minivan relationship. At the garage, I sat and knit while the van endured a battery of tests and difficult moments. Finally, I was waved to the van's side by the mechanic on duty.

With dismay and shock showing clearly on his face, the mechanic showed me the display on the diagnostic computer that was connected to my minivan.

My very seriously ill 1987 minivan was claiming on the glow of the digital readout to be a perfectly healthy 1990 sports car. I was standing there, wondering alternately where you can get your car therapy for denial and how the hell I was going to get to Knit Night when it hit me.

Denial, anger, bargaining, depression, and acceptance are the five stages of death, according to Dr. Elisabeth Kübler-Ross. The van had been working through its terminal illness. It was finally over between us. I took my yarn from the trunk, left the wheel warmer as a memento, bowed my head, and gently touched the fender to say good-bye.

Ten Knitting Tragedies
(from Which There Is Little Return)

1. Puppy. Lace. Thirteen hundred yards of silk in a ball. Please don't make me speak of it.
2. Moths. We can pretend all we like, but the odds are exceptionally good that moths are like knitters' herpes. Nobody wants to admit they have them, and once you've got them, you have them forever even if you're just waiting for the next outbreak.
3. Finally succeeding in teaching all your children to knit, only to discover that this means they want your stash.
4. A sweater going into the wash human-sized and coming out doll-sized. (This is especially painful if you weren't the one who put it in the wash or if, like many knitters, you no longer play with dolls, no matter how well-dressed.)
5. Deciding to survey your lifetime stash accumulation and realizing it's a horrible tragedy that the period of your life in which you had the most money to spend on yarn (and did spend on yarn) also appears to be the time that you had the least amount of taste.

6. Watching as you gently immerse your elegant new sweater, fresh off the needles, into its first gentle bath and feeling the horror spread over you as the deep red yarn of the yoke bleeds—no, hemorrhages—most of its ruby dye into the pristine ivory white of the body.

7. Ripping a sock back because it's too long, then reknitting the toe and finding it too short, then doing it again to make it longer, then running out of yarn on the second one because it turns out you don't have enough yarn for long socks and need to make short ones.

8. Dropping one needle somewhere in the parking lot of the Marine Atlantic ferry dock in Port aux Basques, Newfoundland, and not noticing until the ship has left port to make its seven-hour crossing to North Sydney, Nova Scotia.

9. Knitting the whole plain body of a sweater that will have a fancy yoke, finishing the boring part that took forever but didn't require you to look at the pattern, then realizing, after ripping up the house for fifteen hours looking for it, that you've probably recycled the pattern in a fit of tidiness.

10. After spending six months knitting your sister a beautiful violet lace cardigan, which is lovingly wrapped under the tree in the next room, you sit in abject horror and depression at Christmas dinner with your family, listening to your very fashion-conscious sister say she would never, ever be caught dead in something as dowdy, out of vogue, and hopeless as a violet lace cardigan.

Dear ~~John~~ Sweater

Dear ~~John~~ Sweater,

I have been struggling with how to tell you this since the episode with the miscrossed cable, and I know that as soon as you read those words, you will know that whatever I'm about to write can't be good, and you're right. I know it can't just be me who has felt a distance develop between us; after all, how could you not feel it, what with the way I've had you rammed into a ratty knitting bag in the back of the hall closet. I know it's been obvious to you that we just weren't finding time to be with each other, and you were right that I have withdrawn from you, both emotionally and physically. I know you blame me for that, what with you being an inanimate object, and I know that when I pulled the needles out of you the other day and used them for something else it was a terrible way to show you how I felt.

I finally decided that as immature and cowardly as it may seem to leave you a note, I just couldn't bring myself to tell you to your face.

I didn't want this to turn into a scene. I tried writing you a casual letter, just a quick "Good-bye and thanks for all the stitches," but I find that I'm too angry, and all the clichés that people write in these letters just didn't ring true. As a matter of fact, they all made me madder.

I thought, when I achieved gauge with your swatch, that it meant we were a good fit, and then, when everything kept working when you were an actual sweater, I developed what was obviously a sense of false confidence about your commitment to me. Achieving simultaneous row and stitch gauge doesn't happen much in this world, let me tell you, and I took it as a sign that you cared. Now that you're just about finished, and you come nowhere close to fitting, I can't help but feel that you lied to me. You're too constraining, and I'd love to be able to look you in the eye and utter the classic line, "It's not you, it's me," but my breasts haven't changed at all while we've been on this journey, my woolly friend. I know, because I measured them again this morning, and since they are exactly the same size and shape they were three weeks ago, that does makes it you . . . not me.

I told myself that in this sort of letter, I'm supposed to write something about how the failure of our relationship doesn't mean anything about your worth as a sweater. I'm supposed to tell you that I'm sure you're right for someone, but I have to tell you, your arms are too damn short, and not just for me. I have shortened the sleeves of every sweater I have ever knitted. Due to the somewhat petite nature of my arms (fine; they are stumpy, I grant you that much), I have whacked four inches off of every pattern I have ever been with. This time (perhaps sensing your duplicitous nature) I only took an inch off. It would piss me off royally if the sleeves were now an inch too short, but it has incensed me to vicious purple wrath that they are actually about five inches too short. This means that they wouldn't have worked even if I just let you be you, and that means that there isn't a woman alive that you're a match for. I'd try to be reassuring, but your future as a garment in a relationship with a human looks bleak.

I'm not going to say, "We could still be friends," because we both know that after the way the armholes went, that's just not going to be possible. I know that I'm the one who said we should try for set-in sleeves, but every time I feel you pinch my underarms and bunch up at the top, I think I've been a fool to try. If I told you once, I told you a hundred times that I can't be in a relationship with a sweater that can't see the way I need sleeve caps to fit into openings, and I can't listen to you tell me again that I just need to work on "ease." Screw it.

I know that part of this has been my fault. I did things with you that I thought I would never do with anyone. Before I met you I knew there was a kind of commitment in knitting that I wasn't emotionally ready for, but then I met you, and something about your deep, strong ribbing made it seem like it was going to be okay. I should have been true to myself and stuck with what I know, but you weren't honest about your bad sweater attitude. The next thing I knew, I was cabling all over the place. I found myself up late, neglecting all the things that I'm responsible for. I know love is a mad, mad place, but when I found myself doing a three-over-three left twist cable without a cable needle, I had to do some deep thinking. I still don't know what about you made me take a chance like that, but I know that I'm the one who's going to have to deal with an unplanned dropped stitch, and frankly, I think my mother was right, and the only way to deal with the risk is abstinence.

Good luck in all your future endeavors. I don't know what your future will hold for you, what with the way I intend to rip you all the way back into balls as soon as I have a stiff drink and stomp on you for three or four hours, but I suppose that maybe you could go back to the yarn store where we met. That alpaca you were snuggling with the first day I saw you might be fool enough to let you back on the shelf.

~~Love,~~ (sorry, don't want to lead you on)
Stephanie

that she was so old that she had maxed out, simply reached an age where she was as old as she was going to get, physically, and it seemed like Helen was just going to cruise along like that forever. Every time I saw her she was very old but very active and busy and caring for her husband, home, and dog. (Helen and Don are the proud owners of "Cricket the perpetual dog," whom they would have you believe has been the same dog for forty-five years. Less perceptive people would fall for it, too, since for forty-five years Helen has been accompanied by a white and brown Jack Russell terrier who can do a multitude of tricks. It wasn't until I was about thirty-five years old myself, and I was telling my children that I remembered playing these same tricks with Cricket when I was a little girl, that I began to suspect something was up. Further thought did reveal that Cricket seemed to improve in physique and perkiness to marked degree every ten to fifteen years—the life span of that breed—and I suddenly realized that Helen and Don might be protecting me and my siblings from a terrible truth.) Helen stayed the same, cruising along giving us four kids five dollars and pairs of woolen mittens each Christmas.

They were good mittens, too. The occasional pair turned up a wee bit scratchy, but after a couple of snowstorms and washings they softened right up and became softer. They were always plain, practical mittens, usually all one color, but every so often a brighter striped pair would turn up. There was a lot of other knitted stuff around then, when we were all little. I didn't get much of it, on account of us kids having a knitting Nana who kept us well covered, but Uncle Don had vests, and there were scarves and hats and knitted ripple afghans from the '70s, and all manner of defense against the Canadian winter, all products of Auntie Helen's needles.

Helen talked about it, too. Once she fondly recalled a twinset she made with a plain sweater underneath and a matching cardigan with rabbit fur trim on top. That set stuck in her mind because Helen thought it was the loveliest thing she had ever owned, and her mother chided her for wasting the money on such fancy wool. I asked her whether she ever knit socks, and she looked at me like I was quite mad. "Of course I did, dear. We all did," was her patient reply. She told me about knitting socks for soldiers during the Second World War, and knitting argyle socks in the '50s because they were a huge fad and all the women were knitting them. I love listening to her talk about knitting. It all comes from a different era, a time when part of her knitting was not just for fun or fashion but because her family needed warm things, and buying them was too expensive. Helen knit from the time she was a little girl, only five or six years old, until sometime in the last few years, though I'm ashamed to say I didn't notice exactly when.

After hovering around the "very old" mark for years and years and years, Helen made a leap toward "ancient," and I started noticing some things. Me being me, I noticed it first in her knitting. Out of the blue, she was knitting nothing but mittens. The same mitten pattern, over and over again. More years went by, and then there were only plain mittens. Helen's age had finally caught up with her, and her eyes were too bad to see patterns any more. She'd taken to just knitting what she could remember how to knit without instructions . . . and that was mittens. When her sight failed further, she knit by touch.

family watched over her and assumed more and more of even the simplest tasks she could no longer do, that they began to notice that her hands had developed a spasm or tremor of some kind. Her old, tired hands never stopped moving, churning restlessly all day, and even some of the time that she drifted in and out of sleep. They all worried, but the doctor and nurse agreed that she was so close to the end that you had to expect this sort of odd thing.

Everyone tried to smooth her over. Everyone tried so hard. They held her hands, they stroked them. The knitter had loved many people well and properly in her life, and she was never left alone in those last days. Family drifted in and out. Came and went. Drank endless pots of coffee and fretted about leaving even for a little while. There was always another pair of hands to soothe hers. Lifting, holding. One by one, her daughters came to her, by themselves and at different times, but each held one of those well-used, thin hands to her face. They pressed their old mother's palms against their cheeks, laying their own hands on top firmly enough to try and keep some of her with them. They inhaled her smell, and then the daughters replaced her hands on the smooth sheet of her bed, and every time her hands were let go, they fluttered back to making the same repetitive movements.

Though she seemed calm in every other way, the family was troubled by this. They thought it was a sign that she wasn't peaceful, and that was all they wanted for her. In the afternoon on a day very close to the end, some of her friends came to see her. They were old too, and they knew that they were saying good-bye, not visiting, and